Law Express

COMPANY LAW

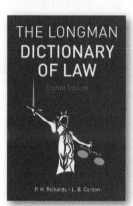
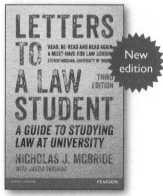

Law**Ex**press

COMPANY LAW

3rd edition

Chris Taylor
Senior Lecturer in Law
Bradford University Law School

PEARSON

Harlow, England • London • New York • Boston • San Francisco • Toronto • Sydney • Auckland • Singapore • Hong Kong
Tokyo • Seoul • Taipei • New Delhi • Cape Town • São Paulo • Mexico City • Madrid • Amsterdam • Munich • Paris • Milan

Pearson Education Limited
Edinburgh Gate
Harlow CM20 2JE
United Kingdom
Tel: +44 (0)1279 623623
Web: www.pearson.com/uk

First published 2009 (print)
Second edition published 2013 (print and electronic)
Third edition published 2015 (print and electronic)

ISBN: 978-1-292-01292-6 (print)
       978-1-292-01815-7 (ePub)
       978-1-292-01338-1 (PDF)
       978-1-292-01310-7 (eText)

British Library Cataloguing-in-Publication Data
A catalogue record for the print edition is available from the British Library

Library of Congress Cataloging-in-Publication Data
Taylor, Chris, author.
   Company law / Chris Taylor, Bradford University. – Third edition.
     p. cm. – (Law express)
   Includes index.
   ISBN 978-1-292-01292-6
   1. Corporation law--England--Outlines, syllabi, etc.   I. Title.
   KD2079.6.T39 2014
   346.42'066–dc23
                          2014001193

ARP impression 98

Print edition typeset in 10/12pt Helvetica Neue LT Std by 35
Print edition printed and bound in Great Britain by Ashford Colour Press Ltd

NOTE THAT ANY PAGE CROSS REFERENCES REFER TO THE PRINT EDITION

Contents

Supporting resources

Visit the *Law Express* series companion website at **www.pearsoned.co.uk/ lawexpress** to find valuable student learning material including:

- A **study plan** test to help you assess how well you know the subject before you begin your revision
- Interactive **quizzes** to test your knowledge of the main points from each chapter
- Sample **examination questions** and guidelines for answering them
- Interactive **flashcards** to help you revise key terms, cases and statutes
- Printable versions of the **topic maps** and **checklists** from the book
- **'You be the marker'** allows you to see exam questions and answers from the perspective of the examiner and includes notes on how an answer might be marked
- **Podcasts** provide point-by-point instruction on how to answer a typical exam question

Also: The companion website provides the following features:

- Search tool to help locate specific items of content
- E-mail results and profile tools to send results of quizzes to instructors
- Online help and support to assist with website usage and troubleshooting

For more information please contact your local Pearson Education sales representative or visit **www.pearsoned.co.uk/lawexpress**

Acknowledgements

Our thanks go to all reviewers who contributed to the development of this text, including students who participated in research and focus groups which helped to shape the series format.

Introduction

Company law is a challenging but interesting area of legal study and one which is increasingly in demand from employers. With the implementation of the Companies Act 2006, many of those involved in the running of companies find themselves having to grapple with the new provisions. For this reason, students who can demonstrate a grasp of the new regulatory framework will have a distinct advantage.

Against this background it is even more important that you are well prepared for the examination and that you understand the most common pitfalls which undermine so many students. As a rule, examinations in company law are often dominated by problem questions and many students do not fully exploit the opportunities which such questions present. Answers which are general, lack supporting authority and which do not offer clear advice to the parties involved will always score badly and so it is vital to adopt a structured approach and to address all of the key issues in a methodical manner.

Essay questions, by contrast, tend to focus on the development of a principle such as limited liability or minority shareholder protection and require not only a statement of the relevant provisions but also analysis of the effectiveness of the law, and an essay which simply recites the section numbers and cases will always underachieve.

It is important to remember that company law is invariably a second- or third-year subject on undergraduate programmes and this means that it will be assessed at a level which requires evidence of analytical ability. That said, the level of analysis required to satisfy that element of the assessment is relatively modest and so even the most basic advice to the parties in a problem question or the most tentative conclusion in an essay will significantly elevate your marks – providing that they are based on relevant legal principles and supported by appropriate authorities.

In comparison to many other areas of legal study, company law is heavily 'statute based', formerly by the Companies Act 1985 and now by the Companies Act 2006.

Remember that this is a revision guide, not a core text, so it can never provide you with the depth of understanding which you will need to excel in examinations and it will be no substitute for attendance at lectures and tutorials, together with structured reading around the various topics. What it can do, however, is to focus your revision on the key areas and highlight those additional points which examiners are looking for. The single most common failing in company law examinations is that students write 'common sense' answers, without sufficient reference to the cases and legal principles. This usually arises from a lack of familiarity with the provisions and an assumption that, if you recognise the general area of law, that will be sufficient. That may be true if a bare pass mark is your aim but, as in any other area of legal writing, there really is no such thing as a free lunch. You need to produce logical, reasoned arguments supported by relevant authorities if you are to achieve the highest grades.

📖 **REVISION NOTE**

Before you begin, you can use the study plan available on the companion website to assess how well you know the material in this book and identify the areas where you may want to focus your revision.

Guided tour

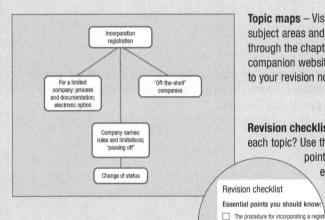

Topic maps – Visual guides highlight key subject areas and facilitate easy navigation through the chapter. Download them from the companion website to pin on your wall or add to your revision notes.

Revision checklists – How well do you know each topic? Use these to identify essential points you should know for your exams. But don't panic if you don't know them all – the chapters will help you revise each point to ensure you are fully prepared. Print the checklists off the companion website and track your revision progress!

Revision checklist

Essential points you should know:

- ☐ The procedure for incorporating a registe
- ☐ The required documentation and the use
- ☐ The role of the Registrar of Companies
- ☐ Issues surrounding the choice of comp
- ☐ The process of re-registration, from

Sample questions with answer guidelines – Practice makes perfect! Read the question at the start of each chapter and consider how you would answer it. Guidance on structuring strong answers is provided at the end of the chapter. Try out additional sample questions online.

▓ Sample question

Could you answer this question? Below is a typical essay question that could arise on this topic. Guidelines on answering the question are included at the end of this chapter, whilst a sample problem question and guidance on tackling it can be found on the companion website.

ESSAY QUESTION

Assess how company law has sought to address the difficulties surrounding pre-incorporation contracts and the effectiveness of the current provisions.

Assessment advice – Not sure how best to tackle a problem or essay question? Wondering what you may be asked? Use the assessment advice to identify the ways in which a subject may be examined and how to apply your knowledge effectively.

ASSESSMENT ADVICE

This topic can appear on examination papers in both essay and problem format and both types of question require a similar treatment. In each case, you need to be able to outline the theoretical problems surrounding pre-incorporation contracts, before moving on to discuss the development of the common law and the uncertainty which surrounded the interpretation of such contracts. Finally, you need to be able to assess the impact of the current statutory provisions.

Key definitions – Make sure you understand essential legal terms. Use the flashcards online to test your recall!

KEY DEFINITION: Objects clause

The clause within the company's constitution which states what is to be the purpose of the company.

Key cases and key statutes –
Identify and review the
important elements of the
essential cases and statutes
you will need to know for your
exams.

KEY STATUTE

Companies Act 2006, se
(1) A contract that purports
the company has not b
contrary, as one made
agent for it, and he i

KEY CASE

Reckitt and Colman Products Ltd v. Borden Inc. and others [1990] 1 All ER 873 (HL)

Concerning: passing off

Facts

A company sold lemon juice in a plastic container shaped like a lemon. Over time it became the best-selling lemon juice. A rival company began selling its lemon juice in a similar container. The first company alleged 'passing off'.

Make your answer stand out – This
feature illustrates sources of further thinking
and debate where you can maximise your
marks. Use them to really impress your
examiners!

✓ Make your answer stand out

The introduction of a statutory procedure for challenging company names by means of the company names adjudicator is a relatively recent development in company law. For further detail which you could include in your answers see Scanlan (2007) and Montagnon and O'Loughlin (2009).

Exam tips – Feeling the pressure? These
boxes indicate how you can improve your
exam performance when it really counts.

✎ EXAM TIP

You can impress the examiner by pointing out that, by the time the case was heard, the debenture had been transferred to a third party: however, this was held to be irrelevant. The third party was equally entitled to the security conferred by the debenture.

Revision notes – Get guidance for effective
revision. These boxes highlight related
points and areas of overlap in the subject,
or areas where your course might adopt
a particular approach that you should check
with your course tutor.

📖 REVISION NOTE

Two of the key statutory exceptions to *Salomon* relate to 'pre-incorporation' contracts, addressed in Chapter 4, and disqualified directors, addressed in Chapter 6. Be sure to include these examples in any answer.

Don't be tempted to . . . – This feature
underlines areas where students most often
trip up in exams. Use them to spot common
pitfalls and avoid losing marks.

! Don't be tempted to . . .

A common failing in company law exams is that students fail to recognise that limited liability, as expressed in *Salomon*, is the accepted position in law. As such, you do not have to prove that limited liability and corporate personality exist – they are our starting point in any question. Having established this point, the question is whether any of the recognised exceptions to *Salomon* will apply.

Read to impress – Focus on these carefully
selected sources to extend your knowledge,
deepen your understanding, and earn better
marks in coursework as well as in exams.

READ TO IMPRESS

Arora, A. (2003) 'Reforming the Company Acts', 5(6) *Finance and Credit Law* 1.

Pike, A. (2008) 'Articles of association and CA 2006', 31(26) *Company Secretary's Review* 201.

Ryan, C. (2008) 'The statutory contract under section 33 of the Companies Act 2006: the legal consequences for banks Pt I', 6 *Journal of International Banking and Finance Law* 304.

Ryan, C. (2008) 'The statutory contract under section 33 of the Companies Act 2006: the legal consequences for banks Pt II', 7 *Journal of International Banking and Finance Law* 360.

Glossary of terms

Glossary – Forgotten the meaning of
a word? This quick reference covers key
definitions and other useful terms.

The glossary is divided into two parts: key definitions and other useful terms. The key definitions can be found within the chapter in which they occur, as well as in the glossary below. These definitions are the essential terms that you must know and understand in order to prepare for an exam. The additional list of terms provides further definitions of

Guided tour of the companion website

Book resources are available to download. Print your own **topic maps** and **revision checklists**!

Use the **study plan** prior to your revision to help you assess how well you know the subject and determine which areas need most attention. Choose to take the full assessment or focus on targeted study units.

'Test your knowledge' of individual areas with quizzes tailored specifically to each chapter. **Sample problem and essay questions** are also available with guidance on writing a good answer.

Flashcards test and improve recall of important legal terms, key cases and statutes. Available in both electronic and printable formats.

'You be the marker' gives you the chance to evaluate sample exam answers for different question types and understand how and why an examiner awards marks.

Download the **podcast** and listen as your own personal Law Express tutor guides you through answering a typical but challenging question. A step-by-step explanation on how to approach the question is provided, including what essential elements your answer will need for a pass, how to structure a good response, and what to do to make your answer stand out so that you can earn extra marks.

All of this and more can be found when you visit **www.pearsoned.co.uk/lawexpress**

Table of cases and statutes

■ Cases

■ Statutes

▮ Statutory Instruments

▮ European Legislation

Companies and other trading structures

Revision checklist

Essential points you should know:

- [ ] There are a number of different trading structures including sole trader, partnership, private limited company and public limited company

- [ ] Each structure has different characteristics which make it more suitable for some businesses than for others

- [ ] The main distinction is between those structures which offer 'limited liability' and those which do not

■ Topic map

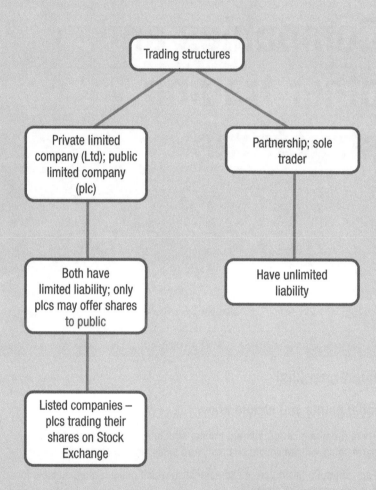

■ Introduction

Just because you have a business does not mean that you have to form a company.

As the name suggests, 'company law' concentrates on the law relating to limited companies; however, this is not the only trading structure available when starting a business. Examiners will want to see that you can recognise when it would be advisable for an individual to register a limited company and when it would not, as this demonstrates that you are familiar with the key attributes of the different trading entities and can assess their relative benefits. For this reason it is not uncommon to see an examination question which asks you to evaluate the different forms that a business can take.

ASSESSMENT ADVICE

Questions on this topic can take the form of essays, which ask you to outline the different trading forms, or problem questions which depict a new business unsure of which trading form to adopt and seeking your advice. In reality, such 'problem' questions are also basically essays, as they require you to set out the different trading structures in exactly the same way but ending with, 'therefore X should be advised to . . .'.

In all cases, you should differentiate clearly between the different structures, paying particular attention to issues of limited liability. It is also important to emphasise the different regulatory burden attached to each, as this is one of the key factors which may influence the choice of which is most appropriate for any particular business.

■ Sample question

Could you answer this question? Below is a typical problem question that could arise on this topic. Guidelines on answering the question are included at the end of this chapter, whilst a sample essay question and guidance on tackling it can be found on the companion website.

PROBLEM QUESTION

Charlie started making garden furniture in his shed as a hobby after he was made redundant two years ago. Over that period, he started selling his furniture to local people and now he has a reputation and a number of orders. Such is the demand that he is seriously considering setting up his own business and the local garden centre has suggested that they would be prepared to order £10,000 worth of furniture a month if Charlie could guarantee delivery. Charlie's cousin Bernie wants to join him in running the business but has told him that they must form a registered company if they are to expand their operation, particularly as they would need to rent larger premises and hire a number of workers if they were to meet the order from the garden centre. This all sounds a little daunting to Charlie and so he seeks your advice.

Advise Charlie on the different forms of trading structure available to him, together with the relative advantages and disadvantages of each.

Trading structures

When starting a business, it is important to select the most appropriate trading structure. The main trading structures available in England and Wales are:

- **sole trader**,
- **partnership**,
- **private limited company** (Ltd),
- **public limited company** (plc) (including 'listed companies'),
- limited liability partnership (LLP).

Each has its own characteristics in relation to three key areas:

- liability,
- ownership and control,
- accountability and regulation.

Sole trader

As the name suggests, the sole trader operates alone and, as such, is the simplest form of trading structure.

Liability

The liability of the sole trader is total. This means that there is no distinction between what belongs to the trader personally and what belongs to the business. Therefore, the debts of the business are the personal responsibility of the trader, who can be pursued by creditors of the business and, in extreme cases, this can lead to the trader being declared bankrupt.

Ownership and control

As the sole trader operates alone, they have complete control over their business and are answerable to no one in the decisions which they take. As the sole trader is the only person involved, they make the decisions and bear the consequences of those decisions. Also, because there is no distinction between the assets of the business and their own personal assets, they legally own all assets of the business and can dispose of them as they wish.

Accountability and regulation

There is very little regulation and official accountability associated with sole trader status. Because they are not registered with Companies House, sole traders are not required to file annual accounts or reports (other than for the payment of income tax and VAT).

Partnership

A partnership arises where two or more people go into business together. There is little or no formality attached to this and a partnership is created simply by agreement between the parties.

KEY STATUTE

Partnership Act 1890, section 1(1)

Partnership is the relation which subsists between persons carrying on a business in common with a view of profit.

Although the minimum number of partners is two, there is no maximum number.

Liability

As with a sole trader, there is no distinction between the assets of the partnership and the assets of the individual partners. Therefore, the partners can be pursued personally for the debts of the partnership.

Ownership and control

A sole trader is accountable only to themselves but partners are accountable to each other and so must agree on decisions affecting the operation of the partnership. Also, whereas a sole trader is the only person affected by their decisions, partners must bear the consequences of each other's decision making. In this way, if one partner makes an error which results in the partnership being sued for damages, each of the partners will be held liable for the money owed.

Accountability and regulation

As with the sole trader, there is relatively little accountability or regulation attached to a partnership and no requirement to file reports and accounts with any official regulator.

Private limited company (Ltd)

The private limited company is the most common trading structure and is the central focus of company law. The company is created by a process of **incorporation**, where the relevant documentation is submitted to Companies House, by the individuals who are setting up the company. These people are known as the **promoters**.

KEY DEFINITION: Promoter

The person or persons who initially incorporate the company. They are the first shareholders and often also the directors. They have the ability to draft the company's memorandum and articles and so can shape the structure and direction of the company.

Liability

Unlike the sole trader and partnership, limited companies (both private and public) own assets which are entirely separate from those of the owners. Therefore, as a general rule, the creditors of the company can only pursue the company's assets to settle any debt. They cannot pursue the personal assets of the owners, who are said to enjoy **limited liability**. This is the most important advantage to forming a limited company and is discussed further in Chapter 3. There is also a category of 'unlimited company', where the company is registered as a separate legal entity but members remain liable for the company's debts in much the same way as a sole trader or partnership. As might be expected, such companies are far less common than limited companies.

Ownership and control

Most limited companies are owned by 'members' who each own a number of shares in the company. For this reason, they are also known as 'shareholders'. Usually, each share has a vote attached to it and so the members are able to vote on important decisions affecting the company, although the day-to-day management of the company is left to the directors. In this way, unlike the sole trader and partnership structures, where ownership and control lies with the same individuals, in a limited company there is a division between ownership (which lies with the shareholders) and control (which lies with the directors). However, it is possible that all of the shareholders of a very small company are also the directors and, following the introduction of the Companies (Single Member Private Limited Companies)

Regulations 1992, it is even possible to have a single person who is both the sole shareholder and the sole director of the company.

One important distinction between limited companies and the sole trader/partnership model is that, for every share the company sells, it also transfers control in the form of votes. In this way, if a sole trader registers their enterprise as a limited company, they will lose ultimate control of the business if they sell shares to other people, as those new members will be able to vote on how the company is run.

! Don't be tempted to . . .

Although companies limited by share are the most common, be aware that it is also possible to have a company limited by guarantee. In such companies, the promoters of the company 'guarantee' to pay a set sum if the company should go into liquidation. Such companies are far less common than those limited by share, which form the overwhelming majority of commercial companies. Be careful not to confuse the two types of company in your answers.

📖 REVISION NOTE

In order to appreciate fully the differences between sole trader/partnership status and limited liability company, you must understand the concepts of '**corporate personality**' and 'limited liability' discussed in Chapter 3. Return to this chapter after you have read these sections.

Accountability and regulation

Unlike a sole trader or partnership, trading by means of a private limited company involves a considerable degree of accountability and regulation. Companies are accountable to their shareholders by means of regular meetings and also by means of a series of registers which the company is required to keep in order to comply with the provisions of the Companies Act 2006 (CA 2006). These include:

- register of members (CA 2006, s. 113);
- register of debenture holders (CA 2006, s. 743);
- register of directors (CA 2006, s. 162);
- register of interests in company shares (CA 2006, s. 808).

In addition to 'internal' accountability to its members, a company is also subject to 'external accountability' to the wider public. This process is supervised by the **Registrar of Companies**.

KEY DEFINITION: Registrar of Companies

The Registrar of Companies, based at Companies House, performs three vital functions relating to the operation of companies in the UK:

- supervising the incorporation and dissolving of limited companies;
- collecting and storing certain information which companies are required to provide under the Companies Act and other legislation;
- making this information available to the public.

Almost every step which a company takes relating to its management and structure must be notified to the Registrar of Companies. Therefore, when answering exam questions, do not forget to consider whether a particular step involves notifying the Registrar.

The two most important pieces of information which a company must regularly supply to the Registrar are the *annual accounts*, which outline the financial position of the company, and the *annual return*, which presents a 'snapshot' of information about the company's directors, shareholders and finances.

 Make your answer stand out

The degree of regulation and accountability placed on companies is the subject of much political debate. Companies complain about the cost of preparing such documentation and the time which it takes to complete. See Spedding (2004). The government has sought to address such concerns by reducing the burden for smaller businesses: for example, by allowing smaller firms to present simplified accounts. The examiner will give credit for recognition of this as an issue for discussion.

Public limited company (plc)

The public limited company is the largest and most complex trading structure. Like the private limited company, it is created by a process of registration but most public companies begin as private companies and are later re-registered to change their status.

The crucial difference between private and public companies is that only the latter may offer shares for sale to the public.

KEY STATUTE

Companies Act 2006, section 755(1)

A private company . . . must not –

(a) offer to the public any securities of the company, or

(b) allot or agree to allot any securities of the company with a view to their being offered to the public.

This confers an enormous advantage on public companies, which can raise vast sums of money by advertising their shares to the public. By contrast, private companies can only raise relatively small sums. In this way, businesses which require massive investment for new products (such as car manufacturers or pharmaceutical companies) are invariably public companies. Another difference between the two types of company is that, whereas there is no minimum capital requirement for a private company, a public company must have a minimum of £50,000 capital (CA 2006, s. 763).

 Make your answer stand out

The fact that there is no minimum capital requirement for private limited companies in England and Wales and only a £50,000 minimum capital requirement for public companies raises questions over whether it is too easy to incorporate a limited company and so take advantage of limited liability. In relation to public companies, such concerns are largely addressed by the stringent approval process but the procedure for the registration of private companies is far less rigorous. A brief mention of this in your answer indicates that you are aware of some of the underlying issues arising from incorporation.

Liability

Like private companies, there is a legal barrier between the assets of public companies and those of the shareholders. This means that the company's creditors can only pursue the assets of the company, and not those of the individual shareholders, who enjoy 'limited liability'. This is vitally important for members of public companies, given the huge sums of money which are involved.

Ownership and control

As with private companies, there is a distinction between ownership (which lies with the shareholders) and control (which lies with the directors). However, unlike private companies, where the directors may also own all of the shares, public companies may have many thousands of shareholders and a relatively small board of directors. Here, the distinction between ownership and control is much more pronounced.

Accountability and regulation

Public companies are subject to a far greater burden of accountability and regulation than private companies. This is imposed primarily by the Companies Act 2006, which allows less freedom to the directors of public companies and which requires more information to be disclosed. The justification for this is the gulf between ownership and control in public companies, which can enable the directors to mislead shareholders more easily, and the huge sums of money involved.

Listed companies

Those public limited companies which wish to trade their shares are 'listed' on the London Stock Exchange. Such **listed companies** are usually the largest trading entities and seek Stock Exchange listing in order to maximise trading in their shares and to attract investors who are reassured by the fact that the company has satisfied the high standards required by the Exchange before it will agree to a company being listed and also by the fact that the company has been able to afford the extremely expensive process.

Liability

Shareholders in listed companies enjoy the same protection of 'limited liability' afforded to members of other public (and private) companies.

Ownership and control

As with other public companies, there is a gulf between the small number of directors and potentially thousands of shareholders and this is even more pronounced in listed companies, where shareholders may live anywhere in the world.

Accountability and regulation

Listed companies are subject to the most rigorous regulatory burden of all, with not only internal accountability to members and external accountability to the Registrar of Companies, but also the additional demands of the Stock Exchange, which imposes its own rules and continuing obligations in order to maintain the integrity and reputation of the market. As a result, listed companies are very carefully monitored and must comply with extensive disclosure requirements. In return, such companies gain access to the markets in order to raise finance and also benefit from the prestige of being a 'listed company'.

Limited liability partnership (LLP)

This is the most recently introduced business structure, following the Limited Liability Partnership Act 2000. Historically, professionals such as solicitors and accountants were compelled to operate within partnerships, rather than companies, in order to increase their vigilance regarding the actions of their partners on the basis that if one partner causes a loss (for example, by their negligence) the others will have to pay. Increasingly, however, firms with large numbers of partners lobbied for a greater degree of personal protection and this culminated in the 2000 Act. Although termed 'partnership', an LLP actually has more in common with a limited company as it must be registered with Companies House, is a separate legal entity and confers a form of limited liability on its members.

Liability

The position of an individual partner within an LLP differs significantly from that of a partner within a traditional partnership. In an LLP, partners are able to limit their liability for general trading debts in much the same way as in a limited company. They cannot, however, restrict their personal liability for their own negligence.

Ownership and control

In this respect an LLP resembles a traditional partnership in that the members enjoy the same day-to-day working relationship.

Accountability and regulation

The regulatory framework applying to LLPs includes elements of company law and elements of partnership law. The LLP must submit annual reports and accounts but there is no requirement for the equivalent of a company director's report.

■ Putting it all together

Answer guidelines

See the problem question at the start of the chapter.

Approaching the question

You can see that this question, although presented as a problem, is really just an essay which requires you to consider the various forms of trading structure and offer some advice on the most appropriate vehicle for this particular business. As such, it is possible to achieve a high mark providing that you adopt a methodical approach and deal with the relevant points one by one, rather than leaping straight to a conclusion. Remember that the examiner will be looking for both description and analysis. You ▶

achieve the first by setting out clearly the characteristics of the various trading structures. You achieve the second by assessing the advantages and disadvantages of each and offering some advice to the person in the scenario.

Important points to include

You should begin this sort of question by recognising that Charlie is currently trading as a sole trader, with no separation between the assets of the business and his personal assets (to appreciate fully the significance of this point you should read about corporate personality and limited liability – see Chapter 3). As the money involved appears to be relatively modest, it seems likely that Charlie could bear the financial blow should the business fail. His cousin Bernie wishes to join him in running the business, which raises the question of whether they should proceed as a partnership or register a limited company. Again, you need to appreciate the significance of limited liability to address this issue fully but it is clear that, as a partnership, Charlie would be potentially liable for any losses which Bernie creates. This makes a private limited company an attractive option, particularly in view of the pending contract with the garden centre which would raise the potential losses should the venture fail. A public or listed company can be dismissed as an option due to the small scale of the venture.

 Make your answer stand out

- State the attributes of each type of trading structure and relate them directly to the facts of the scenario.
- Do not simply reject the options of public limited company and listed company – explain why they are not applicable in this case.
- Remember to offer some form of conclusion or advice to the parties – this is the point of the question!

READ TO IMPRESS

Dance, M. (2002) 'Limiting personal liability in business: sole trader, partnership or limited liability company?', 3 *Due Diligence and Risk Management 1* 22.

Haywood, J. (2010) 'LLP members: how limited is your liability? Part 1', 9 *Journal of International Banking and Financial Law* 546.

Mather, J. (2010) 'LLP members: how limited is your liability? Part 2', 10 *Journal of International Banking and Financial Law* 587.

Spedding, L.S. (2004) 'Red tape and the impact on small business, Part I', 3(5) *Advising Business.*

See the following websites for additional information:

www.businesslink.gov.uk

www.companieshouse.gov.uk

www.pearsoned.co.uk/lawexpress

 Go online to access more revision support including quizzes to test your knowledge, sample questions with answer guidelines, podcasts you can download, and more!

Incorporation

2

Revision checklist

Essential points you should know:

- [ ] The procedure for incorporating a registered company in England and Wales
- [ ] The required documentation and the use of electronic incorporation
- [ ] The role of the Registrar of Companies in this process
- [ ] Issues surrounding the choice of company name
- [ ] The process of re-registration, from one form of company to another

■ Topic map

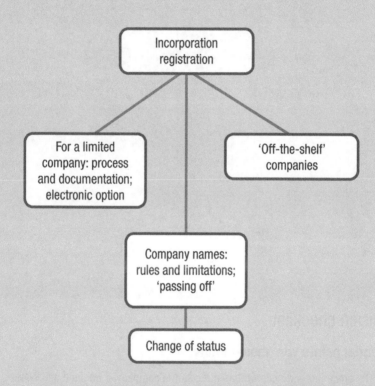

■ Introduction

Companies are not made, they are 'incorporated' and this has to be done in a certain way.

As we saw earlier (in the previous chapter), the private limited company is the most common trading structure for businesses in England and Wales. It also requires a degree of formality which sole trader and partnership status does not. Whereas a person can simply decide to operate as a sole trader and two or more people can simply agree to form a partnership, a limited company does not exist in law until it has been created by a process of 'incorporation' (also known as 'registration' due to the fact that companies are known more formally as 'registered companies'). The procedure for incorporation is laid down in statute and must be followed. For this reason, it must also be understood by students of company law.

ASSESSMENT ADVICE

It is unlikely that you would face an examination question entirely on the topic of incorporation, although it could well feature as an aspect of a larger problem.

As with the previous topic (forms of trading structure), an essay question could ask you simply to outline the incorporation procedure. Similarly, a problem question could depict a new business unsure of how to incorporate a company and seeking your advice or, alternatively, the directors of a private limited company who wish to re-register the company as a public company. Once again, such 'problem' questions are also basically essays with an element of advice at the end. It is also easy for examiners to include some reference to company names in such questions to test your knowledge of this topic.

In all cases, you should adopt a step-by-step approach towards the procedure and make sure that your answer is supported by reference to the relevant provisions. The examiner will be looking for a clear, methodical explanation and this should be your goal!

■ Sample question

Could you answer this question? Below is a typical problem question that could arise on this topic. Guidelines on answering the question are included at the end of this chapter, whilst a sample essay question and guidance on tackling it can be found on the companion website.

■ Incorporating a limited company

The procedures for incorporating a limited company are contained in Part 2 of CA 2006.

KEY STATUTE

Companies Act 2006, section 7(1)

A company is formed under this Act by one or more persons –

(a) subscribing their names to a memorandum of association, and

(b) complying with the requirements of this Act as to registration.

It should be noted that section 7 allows a single person to incorporate a company.

The registration process

In order to register the company, certain documentation must be sent to the Registrar of Companies. The necessary documentation is listed in CA 2006, section 9 and includes the **memorandum of association** (which will be considered in Chapter 5) and the application for registration, which must state the following:

■ the company's proposed name;

■ whether the company's registered office is to be situated in England, Wales, Scotland or Northern Ireland;

■ whether the liability of the members of the company is to be limited and, if so, whether by shares or by guarantee;

■ whether the company is to be a private or a public company.

The application must also contain:

- a statement of capital and initial shareholdings (for a company limited by shares) or a statement of guarantee (for companies limited by guarantee);
- a statement of the company's proposed officers;
- a statement of the intended address of the company's registered office;
- a copy of any proposed **articles of association** (also considered in Chapter 5).

In addition, CA 2006, section 13 also requires the promoters to provide a 'statement of compliance' which declares that the relevant statutory provisions have been complied with.

If the Registrar is satisfied with the documentation provided then he will register the company (s. 14) and issue a certificate of incorporation (s. 15). This signifies that the company is legally created and the date of the certificate is seen as conclusive evidence of valid incorporation. The Registrar must also publish notice of the issue of the certificate of incorporation in the *Gazette* (s. 1064). Note that it is now also possible to register a company electronically.

✎ EXAM TIP

Publication of company information in the *Gazette* is usually ignored by students so you can emphasise your wider knowledge of the topic by drawing attention to this requirement and linking it to the wider disclosure obligation under section 1078 (which implements Article 3 of the First Council Directive 68/151/EEC (the First Company Law Directive)). This applies to a huge range of material, but the examiner will give you credit for simply recognising the existence of such an obligation.

'Off the shelf' companies

In addition to the above procedure, it is also possible to purchase a pre-registered company **'off the shelf'** and then alter the relevant particulars of the company. Such companies are registered in bulk by agencies which specialise in their sale.

■ Company names

There are a number of restrictions relating to the choice of company name, all of which are aimed at preventing third parties from being misled as to the company they are dealing with. These provisions are to be found in the Companies Act 2006.

Indication of company type

A company must use the correct title to indicate clearly the nature of the trading structure.

Companies Act 2006, sections 58(1) and 59(1)

58 Public limited companies

(1) The name of a limited company that is a public company must end with 'public limited company' or 'plc'.

59 Private limited companies

(1) The name of a limited company that is a private company must end with 'limited' or 'Ltd'.

Prohibited names

Under CA 2006, section 53 a company name cannot be registered which, in the opinion of the Secretary of State, would be offensive or which would constitute an offence.

Names requiring approval of the Secretary of State

Under CA 2006, section 54 approval is required for a company name which is likely to suggest a connection with the government, a local authority or a public body. The Company and Business Names Regulations 1981 (as amended) contains a long list of terms which also require such consent before they can be incorporated into a company name.

Category	Examples
Words which imply national or international pre-eminence	'British', 'England', 'Irish', 'Welsh', 'Scottish', 'National', 'European'
Words which imply business pre-eminence	'Association', 'Institution', 'Board', 'Council', 'Authority', 'Society'
Words which imply specific objects or functions	'Post Office', 'Stock Exchange', 'Trade Union'
Others	'Charity', 'Dental', 'Health Service', 'Police', 'University'

There is a further category of restricted names, the use of which is restricted by Act of Parliament. Permission for their use must be sought from the relevant professional body.

Restricted term	Relevant statute
'Architect'	Architects Act 1997
'Building Society'	Building Societies Act 1986
'Olympic'	Olympic Symbol etc. (Protection) Act 1995
'Red Cross'	Geneva Conventions Act 1957

Existing names

A company cannot register a name which is already on the Register of Companies.

KEY STATUTE

Companies Act 2006, section 66(1)

Name not to be the same as another in the index

(1) A company must not be registered under this Act by a name that is the same as another name appearing in the registrar's index of company names.

The Secretary of State may also order a company to change its name if it appears to be too similar to an existing name on the Register.

Challenges to names

In addition to the powers of the Secretary of State, it is also possible for another business to challenge the use of a name by means of the common law action of **passing off**.

KEY DEFINITION: Passing off

An action alleging that the defendant has 'passed off' their goods, services or business as that of the claimant, thereby taking advantage of the reputation or goodwill attached to the claimant's business.

Reckitt and Colman Products Ltd v *Borden Inc. and others* [1990] 1 All ER 873 (HL)

Concerning: passing off

Facts

A company sold lemon juice in a plastic container shaped like a lemon. Over time it became the best-selling lemon juice. A rival company began selling its lemon juice in a similar container. The first company alleged 'passing off'.

Legal principle

Held: this was passing off. The similarity to the original packaging of the successful product constituted a misrepresentation which deceived the public into a mistaken belief regarding the product people were buying. Lord Jauncey: 'it is not essential to the success of a passing-off action that the defendant should misrepresent his goods as those of the plaintiff. It is sufficient that he misrepresents his goods in such a way that it is a reasonably foreseeable consequence of the misrepresentation that the plaintiff's business or goodwill will be damaged.'

In this case, the House of Lords set out that an action for passing off required there to be:

■ goodwill or reputation attached to the goods or services which leads the public to recognise them as associated with the claimant;

■ a misrepresentation by the defendant which is likely to cause the public to believe that the defendant's goods or services are those of the claimant;

■ the likelihood of damage as a result of this mistaken belief.

Challenges under CA 2006

The 2006 Act introduces a statutory mechanism by which a company may be challenged on the use of a name.

Companies Act 2006, section 69

Objection to company's registered name

(1) A person ('the applicant') may object to a company's registered name on the ground –

   (a) that it is the same as a name associated with the applicant in which he has goodwill, or

   (b) that it is sufficiently similar to such a name that its use in the United Kingdom would be likely to mislead by suggesting a connection between the company and the applicant.

The Act also empowers the Secretary of State to appoint 'company names adjudicators' to assess such claims and, when a case is proved, order the offending company to change its name.

 Make your answer stand out

The introduction of a statutory procedure for challenging company names by means of the company names adjudicator is a relatively recent development in company law. For further detail which you could include in your answers see Scanlan (2007) and Montagnon and O'Loughlin (2009).

■ Changing the status of a company

The fact that a business may initially be registered as a particular type of company does not mean that it cannot later change, and the two most common transitions are between private and public limited companies. We have seen that it is possible to incorporate as a public limited company, although most public companies begin as private companies and are later re-registered. Similarly, it is possible for a public company to re-register as a private company. As might be expected, there is a procedure to be followed in each case and the company must be issued with a new certificate of incorporation to reflect its new status.

Private to public company

Once it has achieved a certain size, a private company may wish to change to a public company in order to offer its shares to the public and, by doing so, vastly increase its ability to raise finance. The procedure for a 'private to public' re-registration is provided by CA 2006, section 90 and the principal requirement is that the members of the company approve the change by means of a special resolution (a three-quarters majority of votes cast). A copy of the resolution must be delivered to the Registrar of Companies, accompanied by proof that the company has the minimum share capital required for a public company.

Public to private company

Just as a private company may wish to become a public company, a public company may wish to revert to the less regulated private company structure. The procedure (under CA 2006, s. 97) is much the same as for a private company wishing to become a public company and the change must also be approved by the members by means of a special resolution. However, as there is no minimum capital requirement for a private limited company, there is no requirement for the company to demonstrate a particular level of capital.

Right of members to object to change

Unlike the change from private to public company, which makes it easier to buy and sell the company's shares, the change from public to private company may disadvantage shareholders by making it more difficult to sell their shares, which may have the effect of depressing the share price.

For this reason, shareholders are able to apply to the court to cancel the proposed change under the procedure set out in CA 2006, section 98. This requires:

- the application to be made within 28 days of the resolution;
- the applicants to hold at least 5 per cent of the value of the company's nominal shares;
- the applicants not to have voted for the change.

Public to listed company

As noted previously, the listing of a public company does not alter its status as a public company but, instead, allows the company to trade its shares on the Stock Exchange, with the enhanced status and financial opportunities which this brings. In return, the company must subject itself to greatly increased regulation (not least in the form of the Stock Exchange 'Listing Rules') which is designed to maintain the credibility of the UK financial markets.

The application process for listing is both complex and expensive. It is supervised, not by the Registrar of Companies (as the status of the company as a public company does not change) but, instead, by the Financial Services Authority (FSA) and the Financial Services and Markets Act 2000. In order to approve an application for listing, the FSA must be satisfied of a number of matters relating to the management and financial position of the company.

Criteria	Requirement
Management	Must have appropriate experience
	Must be free from conflicts of interest
Financial position	Must have filed accounts for three years
	Must have 'sufficient working capital'

In addition, the company must have an approved 'sponsor' financial institution which advises the applicant company and supplies information on the company to the FSA. This sponsor company risks penalties if it fails to perform this function properly.

Emphasise in your answers that you know the difference between public and listed companies, as many students treat the two as the same. An awareness of the role of the FSA and the process of applying for listing will always attract extra marks – providing that it is relevant to the question!

■ Putting it all together

Answer guidelines

See the problem question at the start of the chapter.

Approaching the question

As with the problem question earlier (in Chapter 1), this has the appearance of a problem question but, in reality, simply asks you to recount the procedures for registration of a limited company, with reference to the particular circumstances of the parties in the scenario. As explained at the beginning of this chapter, rather than a question on incorporation alone, this is more likely to form one element of a larger problem question (possibly on the issues of corporate personality and limited liability addressed in the next chapter). You will note that there is also a reference to company names which is quite common in questions of this type.

Important points to include

You should begin by assessing the question of whether Sunil actually needs to register a limited company. On the facts, this would appear to be a wise move, as the financial risk which he faces appears to be increasing (this should be linked to the issue of limited liability in Chapter 3). Having decided that this is an appropriate course of action, the precise form of company should be considered. Clearly a public limited company is not feasible or necessary, given the modest scale of the venture, therefore a private limited company would appear to be the most practical solution. From here, it is a straightforward process of listing the information which must be delivered to the Registrar of Companies, as outlined in this chapter.

On the question of the proposed name for the company, 'PC Worlds' is clearly very similar to 'PC World' and so the Registrar of Companies may well refuse to register it. You should also mention the possibility of an action for passing off and the new procedures under CA 2006, section 69.

▶

Make your answer stand out

- Make specific reference to the role of the Registrar of Companies, both in supervising the registration process and (equally importantly) the ongoing supervision of the company.

- Remember to mention the role of the *Gazette* and the requirement for the Registrar to publish notification of registration.

- Emphasise the importance of the certificate of incorporation as conclusive proof that the company has been legally registered.

READ TO IMPRESS

Baker, M. (2001) 'On the register', 25(13) *Company Secretary's Review* 104.

Briault, C. (1999) 'The rationale for a single national financial services regulator', 1(6) *Journal of International Financial Management* 249.

Bridges, C. (2008) 'Statutory procedures', 31(26) *Company Secretary's Review* 208.

(Comment) (2001) 'Two tier company formation system due in spring', 71(11) *Jordan's Journal*.

Little, S. (2002) 'Statutory procedures: re-registration of companies (Part II)', 26(8) *Company Secretary's Review* 64.

Montagnon, R. and O'Loughlin, A. (2009) 'The company names tribunal', 33(7) *Company Secretary's Review* 54.

Scanlan, G. (2007) 'The company names adjudicator – a new regime – new principles?', 28(6) *Company Lawyer* 172.

www.companieshouse.gov.uk

www.pearsoned.co.uk/lawexpress

 Go online to access more revision support including quizzes to test your knowledge, sample questions with answer guidelines, podcasts you can download, and more!

Limited liability and corporate personality

3

Revision checklist

Essential points you should know:

☐ The significance of the decision in *Salomon* v *Salomon & Co. Ltd* [1897] AC 22 (HL)

☐ The theoretical justification for the concept of corporate personality

☐ The consequences of corporate personality and limited liability

☐ Exceptions to *Salomon* – 'lifting the veil'

■ Topic map

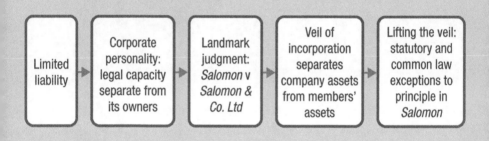

Introduction

Of all the principles of company law, none is more important than corporate personality.

We have already mentioned the principles of limited liability and corporate personality and now we must consider them in more detail. The principles are interrelated and, together, they represent the fundamental basis for company law in England and Wales.

ASSESSMENT ADVICE

The topic appears on almost every company law examination, either as a question in its own right or as an aspect of a larger problem question.

Essay questions

Essay questions tend to ask for a consideration of the principle in *Salomon* and the exceptions to the general rule which are usually referred to as 'lifting the veil'.

Problem questions

Problem questions usually focus on a creditor seeking their money on the liquidation of a company and require you to consider particular exceptions to the rule, either under statute or the common law.

In all cases, you must be able to state clearly the principle of corporate personality as expressed in *Salomon* and outline the exceptions which have been recognised by the courts and by statute. On this topic more than any other, the examiner will want to see a clear grasp of the principles.

Sample question

Could you answer this question? Below is a typical essay question that could arise on this topic. Guidelines on answering the question are included at the end of this chapter, whilst a sample problem question and guidance on tackling it can be found on the companion website.

ESSAY QUESTION

The principle established in *Salomon* v *Salomon Ltd* continues to underpin company law in England and Wales; however, the courts are prepared to ignore the veil of incorporation in order to prevent abuse. Assess the circumstances in which the veil of incorporation may be ignored and the effectiveness of such exceptions to the general rule.

Limited liability

Earlier (in Chapter 1) we made the distinction between two groups of trading structures: those (sole trader and partnership) where there is no distinction between the assets of the owners and the business when faced with claims from creditors, and those (private and public limited companies) where the assets of the owners and the business are entirely separate, thereby protecting the personal assets of the owners from the claims of the company's creditors. Another way of expressing this is that, in the first category, the liability of the owners is 'unlimited' whereas, in the second category, it is 'limited'. The availability of 'limited liability' is one of the most important incentives to set up a company.

KEY STATUTE

Insolvency Act 1986, section 74(2)(d)

In the case of a company limited by shares, no contribution is required from any member exceeding the amount (if any) unpaid on the shares in respect of which he is liable as a present or past member.

This means that the only money for which the shareholders may be pursued is any amount which remains unpaid on any shares which have been bought 'partly paid'. Therefore, under normal circumstances, even if the company's debts run to millions of pounds the shareholders cannot be asked to pay more.

In a company limited by guarantee, the amount which members must pay is the sum which they agreed (or 'guaranteed' to pay) when the company was incorporated.

The incentive of limited liability

For those wishing to invest in companies, the assurance that their liability will be limited is a powerful incentive as it means that entrepreneurs can form companies safe in the knowledge that, if the company fails, their personal assets will be safe. This can be contrasted with the sole trader or member of a partnership, who may find themselves declared bankrupt as creditors pursue claims against them.

Make your answer stand out

Although limited liability protects the owners of companies, it does little to help the company's creditors and customers who, ultimately, bear the losses when the company fails. By contrast, the owners can, effectively, walk away from the debts and then set up a similar company, sometimes from the same premises. Such 'phoenix companies' have a clear potential for fraud and there are concerns that it is too easy for incompetent or dishonest business owners to misuse limited liability. For a discussion of some of the issues, see Griffiths (2006).

■ Corporate personality

The concept of limited liability requires a distinction to be made between the assets of the individual shareholder and the assets of the company itself. For the company to be able to own its assets it must have a legal capacity separate from its owners. This is known as corporate personality.

KEY DEFINITION: Corporate personality

The separate legal status of a registered company which provides it with an identity which is separate from that of its members, shareholders and employees.

Salomon v *Salomon & Co. Ltd*

The principle of a separate corporate personality was acknowledged by the House of Lords in the following landmark judgment.

KEY CASE

Salomon v *Salomon & Co. Ltd* **[1897] AC 22 (HL)**

Concerning: corporate personality

Facts

Salomon had for many years made boots and shoes as a sole trader before deciding to register the business as a limited company. The vast majority of the shares were held by Salomon and one share each held by six other members of his family. He then sold his business to the company. This was paid for by the company paying cash to Salomon and his family and by a secured debenture (i.e. a debt) of £10,000 to Salomon personally. When the company failed, the liquidators argued that the ▶

debenture (which would take priority over the other debts) was invalid as Salomon and the company were effectively one and the same and so the debenture represented a debt to himself, which was impossible in law.

Legal principle

Held: the House of Lords held that the debenture still took priority over the other debts of the company as it was a separate legal entity, completely distinct from its members. Therefore, it could owe money to its members and, accordingly, the debenture in favour of Salomon was valid. Lord Herschell: 'It is to be observed that both courts treated the company as a legal entity distinct from Salomon and the then members who composed it, and, therefore, as a validly constituted corporation.'

Salomon remains the single most important decision in company law. As such, you *must* be able to explain both the facts and the significance of the case.

✎ EXAM TIP

You can impress the examiner by pointing out that, by the time the case was heard, the debenture had been transferred to a third party: however, this was held to be irrelevant. The third party was equally entitled to the security conferred by the debenture.

Effects of corporate personality

Although limited liability is the most important consequence of corporate personality, there are others:

- The company can sue and be sued in its own right.
- The company can be a party to contracts (e.g. to buy and sell goods and to employ staff).
- The company can continue to function after the death of a shareholder.

KEY CASE

Macaura v *Northern Assurance Co.* [1925] AC 619 (HL)

Concerning: corporate personality and insurance

Facts

Macaura sold all of the timber on his estate to a company. He owned almost all of the shares in the company. He insured the timber in his own name but, when the timber was destroyed in a fire, the insurance company refused to pay him, claiming that the timber belonged, not to him, but to the company.

Legal principle

Held: the House of Lords held that the insurance company was correct. The policy would only be valid if the timber belonged to Macaura. However, as it belonged to the company, only the company could insure it. Lord Sumner: 'It is clear that the appellant had no insurable interest in the timber described. It was not his. It belonged to the company.'

KEY CASE

Lee v *Lee's Air Farming Ltd* **[1961] AC 12 (PC)**

Concerning: shareholder director as employee

Facts

Lee owned all but one of the company's shares and was a director. He was killed in a work-related accident but the company's insurers refused to pay compensation as they claimed he could not be an employee of the company. As he owned so much of the company this would amount to him making a contract with himself.

Legal principle

Held: the House of Lords held that, on the basis of *Salomon*, there was nothing to prevent the company (as a separate legal entity) from employing Lee. Therefore, his estate was entitled to compensation. Viscount Simonds: 'The company and the deceased were separate legal entities.'

The 'veil of incorporation'

The law recognises a separation between the assets of the company and those of the members. The barrier between the two has become known as the **veil of incorporation**.

■ Lifting the veil

There are a number of instances where the courts are prepared to ignore the veil of incorporation and hold members personally liable for the debts of the company. Such exceptions to the general principle in *Salomon* are known as 'lifting the veil' and can be found in both statute and common law. There are, however, two common features to all of the recognised exceptions:

■ They are designed to prevent the protection of limited liability being abused to perpetrate fraud or other wrongdoing.

■ They will only apply to members of the company who actually created the situation (i.e. directors).

> **!** Don't be tempted to . . .
>
> A common failing in company law exams is that students fail to recognise that limited liability, as expressed in *Salomon*, is the accepted position in law. As such, you do not have to prove that limited liability and corporate personality exist – they are our starting point in any question. Having established this point, the question is whether any of the recognised exceptions to *Salomon* will apply.

Statutory exceptions

> **□ REVISION NOTE**
>
> Two of the key statutory exceptions to *Salomon* relate to 'pre-incorporation' contracts, addressed in Chapter 4, and disqualified directors, addressed in Chapter 6. Be sure to include these examples in any answer.

Fraudulent trading

One obvious example of conduct which might lead the court to ignore the veil of incorporation is where the company has been created or managed in order to commit fraud.

> **KEY STATUTE**
>
> **Insolvency Act 1986, section 213**
>
> If in the course of the winding up of a company it appears that any business of the company has been carried on with intent to defraud creditors of the company or creditors of any other person, or for any fraudulent purpose. . . . The court, on the application of the liquidator may declare that any persons who were knowingly parties to the carrying on of the business in the manner above-mentioned are to be liable to make such contributions (if any) to the company's assets as the court thinks proper.

The fact that the law will not allow companies and limited liability to be used to commit fraud is unsurprising but it should be noted that fraud is often difficult to prove and requires evidence of real dishonesty.

KEY CASE

Re Patrick Lyon Ltd **[1933] All ER Rep 590 (Ch)**

Concerning: fraud

Facts

A director of the company carried on the business and delayed liquidation of the company for six months after the issue of certain debentures to himself in order to deprive the unsecured creditors of the company of the right to challenge the debentures under section 266 of the Companies Act 1929.

Legal principle

Held: Maugham J: 'I will express the opinion that the words "defraud" and "fraudulent purpose", where they appear in the section in question, are words which connote actual dishonesty involving, according to current notions of fair trading among commercial men, real moral blame.'

Note that the above decision concerned the earlier comparable provisions under the Companies Act 1929.

Wrongful trading

KEY STATUTE

Insolvency Act 1986, section 214

(1) If in the course of the winding up of a company it appears that subsection (2) of this section applies . . . the court, on the application of the liquidator, may declare that that person is to be liable to make such contribution (if any) to the company's assets as the court thinks proper.

(2) This subsection applies in relation to a person if –

    (a) the company has gone into insolvent liquidation,

    (b) at some time before the commencement of the winding up of the company, that person knew or ought to have concluded that there was no reasonable prospect that the company would avoid going into insolvent liquidation, and

    (c) that person was a director of the company at that time.

KEY CASE

Re Produce Marketing Consortium Ltd **[1989] BCLC 520 (Ch)**

Concerning: wrongful trading

Facts

The directors of a fruit importing company had continued to trade, despite their company being technically insolvent, in the hope of 'turning the corner'. Their intentions had been honest but they had ignored warnings from the company's auditors concerning the company's financial position.

Legal principle

Held: the directors would be forced to contribute to the company's debts. Knox J: 'This was a case of failure to appreciate what should have been clear rather than a deliberate course of wrongdoing . . . [however] the fact that there was no fraudulent intent is not of itself a reason for fixing the amount at a nominal or low figure.'

 Make your answer stand out

Although the basic principles of sections 213 and 214 are easily understood, the courts have grappled with their precise application and so, rather than merely stating the provisions, include some reference to these conceptual debates. See Keay (2006) and Fidler (2001).

Common law exceptions

'Sham' or 'façade' companies

The courts have been prepared to lift the veil of incorporation where it is deemed that the company has been used as a 'sham' or 'façade' to hide another, dishonest purpose.

KEY CASE

Gilford Motor Co. Ltd v *Horne* **[1933] Ch 935 (CA)**

Concerning: sham/façade companies

Facts

The defendant was formerly managing director of the claimant company and was subject to a covenant not to approach clients of the company after his employment had ended. After leaving the company, he incorporated a company with his wife and used the company to approach the customers of his former employers.

Legal principle

Held: the defendant had set up the company, not as a genuine business, but rather as a 'sham' or 'façade' to hide his intention to break the covenant with his former employers. This was an abuse of corporate personality. Farwell J: 'I am quite satisfied that this company was formed as a device, a stratagem, in order to mask the effective carrying on of a business of Mr EB Horne.'

KEY CASE

Jones v *Lipman* [1962] 1 All ER 442 (Ch)
Concerning: sham/façade companies

Facts

The defendant agreed to sell a plot of land to the claimant but, before completion, he transferred the land to a company of which he and a partner were sole shareholders and directors. He claimed to be unable to complete the original sale on the basis that he no longer owned the land as it belonged to the company as a result of the transfer.

Legal principle

Held: the company was a 'sham' or 'façade' to prevent having to honour the agreement to transfer the land. Russell J: 'The defendant company is the creature of the first defendant, a device and a sham, a mask which he holds before his face in an attempt to avoid recognition by the eye of equity.'

Groups of companies

In the same way as a person can own a company and be separate from it by means of the doctrine of corporate personality, so can another company and it is increasingly common for one company (known as a 'holding company') to set up another (known as a 'subsidiary company') to take advantage of the principle of limited liability. A successful company faced with a risky business venture may choose to incorporate a separate company to exploit the opportunity safe in the knowledge that, should it fail, only the assets of the subsidiary company can be used to satisfy its debts, leaving the holding company safe. In this way, it is not uncommon for large groups of companies to be owned by the same 'parent company'.

Despite this legitimate use of corporate personality to reduce risk, the courts have been prepared to ignore the corporate veil and treat the holding and subsidiary companies as one and the same. However, this is only under very particular circumstances and the approach adopted by the courts has been far from consistent.

✎ EXAM TIP

The application of *Salomon* to groups of companies is an important emerging area and examiners will be impressed if you can show a knowledge of the key decisions. However, many students fail to distinguish between the various decisions and this undermines their answers. This is an area where the courts have adopted different views at different times and you need to emphasise this when writing on the topic.

It is possible to trace the development of this area in the following decisions.

KEY CASE

The Albazero [1977] AC 774 (HL)

Concerning: corporate personality and groups of companies

Facts

A shipment of oil belonging to one company was transferred to another company during its voyage from South America to Europe. Both companies were entirely owned by the same 'parent' company. After the transfer of ownership, the ship sank and the cargo was lost. When the first company tried to claim for the loss, the shipowners argued that the second company was the true owner of the oil and it could not claim because the limitation period on such claims had expired. Therefore neither company could claim.

Legal principle

Held: Roskill LJ: 'each company in a group of companies . . . is a separate legal entity possessed of separate legal rights and liabilities so that the rights of one company in a group cannot be exercised by another company in that group even though the ultimate benefit of the exercise of those rights would [be] to the same person or corporate body'.

However, in other cases, the courts have adopted a more liberal view.

KEY CASE

Smith, Stone & Knight Ltd v *Birmingham Corporation* [1939] 4 All ER 116 (KB)

Concerning: single economic entity

Facts

SSK, a paper manufacturing company, acquired a waste paper business and registered it as a subsidiary company. The parent company held all the shares except five, each of which was held by its directors. The profits of the new company were treated as profits of the parent company, which exercised total control over the activities of the subsidiary company. When the local authority exercised its powers of compulsory purchase to take the land occupied by the subsidiary company, the parent company claimed compensation for disruption to its business. However, the council argued that the proper claimant was the subsidiary company, which was a separate legal entity.

Legal principle

Held: that possession by a separate legal entity was not conclusive. As the subsidiary company was not operating on its own behalf but rather on behalf of the parent company, the parent company was able to claim compensation. Atkinson J: 'the business belonged to the claimants; they were, in my view, the real occupiers of the premises. If either physically or technically the waste company was in occupation, it was for the purposes of the service it was rendering to the claimants.'

KEY CASE

DHN Food Distributors Ltd v *Tower Hamlets London Borough Council* **[1976] 1 WLR 852 (CA)**

Concerning: single economic entity

Facts

DHN was a parent company, owning two subsidiaries. One of the companies owned a plot of land from which the other company ran a fleet of lorries to deliver goods for DHN. On the compulsory purchase of the land, the question arose as to which company could claim for disruption to its business.

Legal principle

Held: although these were separate companies, they could be regarded as a 'single economic entity'. Denning MR: 'This group is virtually the same as a partnership in which all the three companies are partners. They should not be treated separately so as to be defeated on a technical point.'

The key factors in determining whether the companies were a 'single economic entity' were:

- the degree of control which the parent company exercised over the activities of the subsidiary company (evidenced by the companies having the same board of directors);
- the complete ownership of all of the shares in the subsidiary company by the parent company.

KEY CASE

Woolfson v *Strathclyde Regional Council* [1978] 2 EGLR 19 (HL)

Concerning: single economic entity

Facts

Limited company 'A' carried on a retail business at a shop comprising five premises. Three of the premises were owned by Woolfson and the other two by another limited company 'B'. Woolfson was the sole director of 'A' and owned 999 shares of the 1,000 issued shares of company 'A', the remaining share being owned by his wife. Woolfson also owned 20 of the 30 issued shares of company 'B', with the other 10 being owned by his wife. All of the shop premises were occupied by a company called M & L Campbell, which sold wedding garments. When the premises were compulsorily acquired by the local authority, both Woolfson and company 'B' jointly sought compensation from the Lands Tribunal which held that they were not entitled to such compensation.

Legal principle

Held: as the company which carried on the business had no control whatever over the owners of the land, they could not be regarded as a single economic entity and so the rule in *Salomon* would apply. Lord Keith: 'The fact of the matter is that Campbell was the occupier of the land and the owner of the business carried on there. Any direct loss consequent on disturbance would fall upon Campbell, not Woolfson.'

Over time, the liberal approach applied in *DHN* has been less popular.

KEY CASE

Adams v *Cape Industries plc* [1990] Ch 433 (CA)

Concerning: single economic entity

Facts

Cape, an English Company, mined asbestos which it sold through a subsidiary company in the UK and another in the USA. The US company was sued by a number of former employees for injuries arising from exposure to its asbestos but, as the company had disposed of its assets in the USA, only a successful action against the UK parent company would secure damages for the claimants.

Legal principle

Held: the law recognises the creation of subsidiary companies and, even though they are under the control of their parent companies, they will generally be treated as separate legal entities with all the rights and liabilities which would normally attach to separate legal entities. Slade LJ: 'Each corporate member of the Cape group had its own well-defined commercial function designed to serve the over-all commercial purpose of mining and marketing asbestos. But that does not constitute a reason why Cape, the parent company, should be treated as present and amenable to be sued in each country in which a subsidiary was present and carrying on business.'

Liability of companies in tort and under the criminal law

One aspect of corporate personality which has caused particular difficulty is the extent to which a company can be held liable in tort and also under the criminal law. The latter is particularly problematic because whereas there is no impediment to a company paying a fine just as an individual would, where the offence is so serious as to warrant imprisonment the doctrine of corporate personality seems less helpful – after all, you cannot put a company in prison. Also, in an offence where *mens rea* must be established, mental state is relevant as the company does not 'think' in the same way as a person does.

In relation to tortious liability, the doctrine of vicarious liability renders the company liable for negligent actions on the part of its employees providing that these were committed in the course of the employment. The situation may be more complex, however, where some knowledge of the circumstances are required. Here the situation resembles that of *mens rea*.

Historically, the courts favoured establishing liability by reference to the decisions of those seen as exercising the 'directing mind and will' of the company. This is also sometimes expressed in terms of the person acting as the 'alter ego' of the company. The decisions of such persons were, in effect, viewed as the decisions of the company and could generate liability accordingly. Conversely, if the decision in question was not made by someone sufficiently senior to constitute the 'directing mind and will' of the company, the company could evade liability.

KEY CASE

Tesco Supermarkets Ltd v *Nattrass* [1971] 2 All ER 127 (HL)

Concerning: liability

Facts

The manager of a supermarket failed to notice that boxes of washing powder had been put on display at a price which was higher than the advertised sale price. This was contrary to the Trade Descriptions Act 1968. The company argued a defence under section 24(1) of the 1968 Act in that the offence arose from the act or default of ▶

'another person' where the company had taken all reasonable precautions and exercised all due diligence to avoid the commission of the offence. The appellant's conviction was upheld by the Divisional Court on the ground that, although the manager was 'another person' within the meaning of the Act, the requirement that the accused must take all reasonable precautions and exercise all due diligence meant not only the accused but also all his servants acting in a managerial or supervisory capacity.

Legal principle

Held: in the case of a limited company, a failure to exercise due diligence on its part required the failure of a director or senior manager who was in actual control of the company's operations and who could, therefore, be identified with the 'controlling mind and will of the company'. Lord Pearson: 'Being the manager of one of the company's several hundreds of shops, [he] could not be identified with the company's ego nor was he an alter ego of the company. He was an employee in a relatively subordinate post. In the company's hierarchy there were a branch inspector and an area controller and a regional director interposed between him and the board of directors.'

This established the 'identification theory', that the decisions of a director can be attributed to the company itself. Note, however, that this may depend on the precise wording of the offence in question.

KEY CASE

Tesco Stores Ltd v ***Brent London Borough Council*** [1993] 2 All ER 718 (QB)
Concerning: liability

Facts

A trading standards officer sent a 14-year-old boy to purchase an '18' video at a Tesco supermarket. A check-out operator sold the video in contravention of the Video Recordings Act 1984. There was a defence under the Act where the defendant 'neither knew nor had reasonable grounds to believe' that the person was underage. Tesco argued that those with the 'directing mind and will' of the company had no knowledge of the boy or his age.

Legal principle

Held: on the true construction of the 1984 Act there was no distinction between a company accused of the offence of supplying a video recording to an underage person and those under its control who physically supplied the video recording. Staughton LJ: 'It is the employee that sells the film at the check-out point who will have knowledge or reasonable grounds for belief. It is her knowledge or reasonable grounds that are relevant. Were it otherwise, the statute would be wholly ineffective in the case of a large company, unless by the merest chance a youthful purchaser were known to the board of directors.'

As indicated previously, there is no difficulty in a company being required to pay a fine under the criminal law. Major difficulties have arisen, however, where a death results in a charge of manslaughter against the company and the courts were required to determine whether the death arose from decisions of the 'controlling mind and will' of the company. In a number of cases this proved to be impossible and so pressure grew for reform.

KEY STATUTE

Corporate Manslaughter and Corporate Homicide Act 2007, section 1

(1) An organisation to which this section applies is guilty of an offence if the way in which its activities are managed or organised –

    (a) causes a person's death, and

    (b) amounts to a gross breach of a relevant duty of care owed by the organisation to the deceased.

(2) The organisations to which this section applies are –

    (a) a corporation;

    (b) a department or other body listed in Schedule 1;

    (c) a police force;

    (d) a partnership, or a trade union or employers' association, that is an employer.

(3) An organisation is guilty of an offence under this section only if the way in which its activities are managed or organised by its senior management is a substantial element in the breach referred to in subsection (1).

(4) For the purposes of this Act –

    (a) 'relevant duty of care' has the meaning given by section 2, read with sections 3 to 7;

    (b) a breach of a duty of care by an organisation is a 'gross' breach if the conduct alleged to amount to a breach of that duty falls far below what can reasonably be expected of the organisation in the circumstances;

    (c) 'senior management', in relation to an organisation, means the persons who play significant roles in –

        (i) the making of decisions about how the whole or a substantial part of its activities are to be managed or organised, or

        (ii) the actual managing or organising of the whole or a substantial part of those activities.

The offence under section 1 of the 2007 Act shifts the emphasis away from decisions made by the 'controlling mind and will' of the company to consider broader questions of the management systems employed by the company. The first successful prosecution for corporate manslaughter under the Act was *R v Cotswold Geotechnical (Holdings) Ltd* [2011] All ER (D) 100 (May).

■ Putting it all together

Answer guidelines

See the essay question at the start of the chapter.

Approaching the question

This type of essay question on corporate personality and 'lifting the veil' appears on almost every company law examination in some form or other. The crucial point to bear in mind is that the examiner is not just looking for a list of the various provisions, but also for some degree of critical evaluation of the effectiveness of both the principle of corporate personality itself and the exceptions to the general rule. Remember that corporate personality, as expressed in *Salomon*, is the starting point and the exceptions should follow (not the other way round).

Important points to include

You should begin by clearly setting out the doctrine of corporate personality and explaining the decision in *Salomon*. This should be followed by an explanation of the effects of limited liability and its attraction to shareholders and directors, together with a description of the 'veil of incorporation'.

Having established the principle of corporate personality you should then address the exceptions to the general rule, which are all based on a desire to prevent the corporate form from being abused. Look at both the statutory and common law exceptions and try not only to state what the exception is but also to offer some view on how effective or otherwise you consider it to be. This is particularly important in relation to areas such as groups of companies where even the courts have struggled to find consistency of approach.

Finally, provide a conclusion which addresses the question and which provides some opinion on the central proposition – the effectiveness of the exceptions.

Make your answer stand out

- Place the doctrine of corporate personality within the wider debate surrounding the availability of limited liability as an incentive to entrepreneurship and risk taking, pointing out that the losses are passed on to creditors and customers.

- Use the example of groups of companies to illustrate how the courts have been prepared to ignore *Salomon* to allow companies to claim compensation, yet allow companies to hide behind corporate personality (as in *Adams*) when the claim is against the company itself.

READ TO IMPRESS

Andrews, G. (2004) 'The veil of incorporation – fiction or façade?', 25(1) *Business Law Review* 4.

Fidler, P. (2001) 'Wrongful trading after *Continental Assurance*', 17(6) *Tolley's Insolvency Law and Practice* 212.

Griffiths, M. (2003) 'Lifting the corporate veil revisited', *Legal Executive* (May) 36.

Griffiths, M. (2006) 'The phoenix syndrome', 156 *New Law Journal* 530.

Keay, A. (2006) 'Fraudulent trading: the intent to defraud element', 35(2) *Common Law World Review* 121.

Moore, M.T. (2006) 'A temple built on faulty foundations: piercing the corporate veil and the legacy of *Salomon* v *Salomon*', *Journal of Business Law* 180.

Tweedale, G. and Flynn, L. (2007) 'Piercing the corporate veil: *Cape Industries* and multinational corporate liability', 8 *Enterprise Society* 268.

www.pearsoned.co.uk/lawexpress

 Go online to access more revision support including quizzes to test your knowledge, sample questions with answer guidelines, podcasts you can download, and more!

Pre-incorporation contracts

4

Revision checklist

Essential points you should know:

☐ What is meant by the term pre-incorporation contract

☐ The reasons why such contracts are legally invalid

☐ The development of the common law in relation to enforcing such contracts

☐ The clarification provided by the Companies Act 1985 and Companies Act 2006

■ Topic map

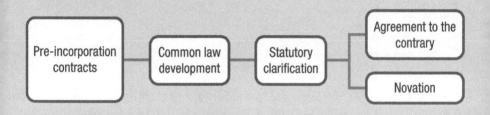

■ Introduction

When is a contract not all that it seems? When it is a pre-incorporation contract.

Having examined the consequences of incorporation and the creation of corporate personality, we now turn to one of the exceptions to the rule in *Salomon* mentioned in the previous chapter. Pre-incorporation contracts are an easy way to find yourself personally liable for the debts of the company. As such, anyone concerned with the management of companies needs to appreciate this area of company law.

ASSESSMENT ADVICE

This topic can appear on examination papers in both essay and problem format and both types of question require a similar treatment. In each case, you need to be able to outline the theoretical problems surrounding pre-incorporation contracts, before moving on to discuss the development of the common law and the uncertainty which surrounded the interpretation of such contracts. Finally, you need to be able to assess the impact of the current statutory provisions.

■ Sample question

Could you answer this question? Below is a typical essay question that could arise on this topic. Guidelines on answering the question are included at the end of this chapter, whilst a sample problem question and guidance on tackling it can be found on the companion website.

ESSAY QUESTION

Assess how company law has sought to address the difficulties surrounding pre-incorporation contracts and the effectiveness of the current provisions.

■ Pre-incorporation contracts

We have seen that the process of incorporation leads to the creation of a legal entity, in the form of the registered company, which enjoys a legal status separate from that of its members. One of the consequences of this 'corporate personality' is that the company has contractual capacity and can make contracts in its own name, such as contracts for the sale and purchase of goods and services, or contracts of employment with its workers. This contractual capacity only exists once the company is incorporated, which raises the question, what happens if the contract is made *before* the incorporation process is completed? This occurs where the promoters (the people who initially register the company) enter into a contract in the company's name with a third party believing (mistakenly) that the company has already been properly incorporated. Such contracts are known as **pre-incorporation contracts** and are legally flawed for a number of reasons.

Capacity

As has already been indicated, the company only comes into legal existence at the moment of incorporation, at which point it gains contractual capacity. It follows, therefore, that prior to incorporation, the company does not legally exist and so cannot have the legal capacity to enter into a valid contract, in the same way that a person does not have contractual capacity for most forms of contract until they reach 18 years of age. This would suggest that a contract made in the name of the company, but before it is incorporated, is void.

Privity

The contractual doctrine of privity provides that only a party to a contract can bring an action under that contract:

A contracts to sell his car to B.

A refuses to honour the agreement.

C tries to enforce the contract against A.

Under the doctrine of privity, C cannot enforce the contract as they were not a party to the original agreement and the same reasoning would apply to a pre-incorporation contract:

The promoters contract (in the name of the non-existent company) to purchase goods.

The company is incorporated.

The third party attempts to sue the company for payment.

Under the doctrine of privity, the third party cannot enforce the contract against the company as it was not a party to the original agreement.

📖 REVISION NOTE

Remember to revise pre-incorporation contracts alongside the other 'lifting the veil' exceptions to the rule in *Salomon* addressed in the previous chapter.

The common law position

If the company cannot be bound to a contract made before it is incorporated, the question then becomes, is the promoter who made the agreement on behalf of the company liable personally under the terms of the contract?

KEY CASE

Kelner v *Baxter* (1866) LR 2 CP 174 (Ct of Common Pleas)

Concerning: pre-incorporation contracts

Facts

The promoters of a company which ran a hotel entered into a contract for the supply of wine before the company was validly incorporated. Before the bill was paid, the company had gone into liquidation and so the suppliers sued the promoters personally. The promoters argued that they had no personal liability under the contract, which was between the supplier and the company.

Legal principle

Held: the promoters were personally liable. Erle CJ: 'as there was no company in existence at the time, the agreement would be wholly inoperative unless it were held to be binding on the defendants personally.'

However, the outcome of cases frequently depended on the precise form of words used in the contract and the manner in which it was signed.

KEY CASE

Newborne v *Sensolid (Great Britain) Ltd* [1954] 1 QB 45 (CA)

Concerning: pre-incorporation contracts

Facts

A contract was agreed for the sale of goods by the company Leopold Newborne (London) Ltd. The document was signed 'Leopold Newborne (London) Ltd' with the signature of Leopold Newborne underneath. At the time of the contract, however, the company had not yet been incorporated. When the goods were delivered, the buyers refused to take delivery and the company sued for breach of contract.

Legal principle

Held: the contract was void. As Leopold Newborne had not signed the contract in a personal capacity, but merely to confirm the identity of the non-existent company, ▶

---

neither the company nor Leopold Newborne personally could be liable for the contract. Lord Goddard CJ: 'This contract purports to be a contract by the company; it does not purport to be a contract by Mr Newborne . . . unfortunate though it may be, as the company was not in existence when the contract was signed there never was a contract.'

Statutory reform

This dependence on the precise wording of the contract created a great deal of uncertainty surrounding such contracts and led to calls for a clear legal position. This came with section 9(2) of the European Communities Act 1972, later replaced by section 36C of the Companies Act 1985 and now by section 51 of the Companies Act 2006.

KEY STATUTE

Companies Act 2006, section 51

(1) A contract that purports to be made by or on behalf of a company at a time when the company has not been formed has effect, subject to any agreement to the contrary, as one made with the person purporting to act for the company or as agent for it, and he is personally liable on the contract accordingly.

✎ EXAM TIP

To add depth and context to the discussion, point out that the statutory provisions regulating pre-incorporation contracts are the result of implementation of the First Company Law Directive 1968, Article 7 of which provides: 'If, before a company being formed has acquired legal personality, action has been carried out in its name and the company does not assume the obligations arising from such action, the persons who acted shall, without limit, be jointly and severally liable therefor, unless otherwise agreed.'

When compared to the previous position under the common law, this does make the position much clearer, as it takes no account of the manner in which the contract was signed. All that matters is that the contract was agreed before the company was incorporated and this is sufficient to leave the promoters personally liable on the contract. The following case was an early example of the courts implementing the new statutory provisions.

KEY CASE

Phonogram v *Lane* [1981] 3 WLR 736 (CA)

Concerning: pre-incorporation contracts under section 51

Facts

Lane, the manager of a pop group, negotiated a recording contract with Phonogram who paid £6,600 to Lane as an advance payment. The intention was to incorporate a company to manage the group and Lane signed the contract 'for and on behalf of' the proposed company. A clause in the agreement stipulated that the money would be repaid to Phonogram in the event that the recording contract was not entered into within one month. The proposed company was never formed and no recording contract was ever entered into.

Legal principle

Held: even though, when the contract was agreed, it was known to both parties that the company was not yet in existence, the defendant was personally liable for it. Furthermore, it did not matter whether the contract had been signed on behalf of the company. Oliver LJ: 'Any such subtle distinctions which might have been raised are rendered now irrelevant by [the Act].'

A related question is whether a person who signs a pre-incorporation contract on behalf of the, as yet, unregistered company is able to sue on the contract.

KEY CASE

Braymist Ltd v *Wise Finance Company Ltd* [2002] EWCA Civ 127 (CA)

Concerning: pre-incorporation contracts

Facts

A solicitor signed a contract for the sale of a plot of land which was to be owned by Braymist Ltd before the company was incorporated. When the vendor of the land refused to complete the sale, the company (once incorporated) and the solicitor sued for damages.

Legal principle

Held: the Act not only provided a remedy for third parties entering into a contract with a company when it was unformed but also imposed obligations on them which were enforceable by the agent of the unformed company. Latham LJ: 'It is submitted . . . that the section is only concerned with the imposition of liability . . . I have great difficulty in accepting this submission.'

Agreement to the contrary and novation

It will be noted that liability under section 51 is 'subject to any agreement to the contrary', i.e. an agreement between the promoter and the other party to the contract that the company, once incorporated, will enter into a new contract with the third party on the same terms (thereby releasing the promoter from personal liability). This process is known as **novation**. However, the courts will require clear evidence before concluding that such a new contract has come into existence (*Bagot Pneumatic Tyre Company* v *Clipper Pneumatic Tyre Company* [1902] 1 Ch 146).

KEY DEFINITION: Novation

The replacement of one contract with another.

Change of company name

What if a company changes its name after the contract is agreed? Is this a pre-incorporation contract?

KEY CASE

Oshkosh B'Gosh Inc. v *Dan Marbel Inc. Ltd* [1989] BCLC 507 (CA)

Concerning: renamed companies

Facts

Egormight Ltd changed its name to Dan Marbel Ltd but, due to delay, it was five years before a certificate of incorporation under the new name was issued. During this time, the company traded under its new name. The claimant supplied goods to the company before the first defendant's name change had been recorded and sought to hold the promoters of the new company liable on the basis of a pre-incorporation contract.

Legal principle

Held: alteration of the company's name could not be taken to reform or reincorporate the company. The company continued to exist but merely under a different name. As such, this could not be a pre-incorporation contract. Nourse LJ: 'the contracts were clearly made by or on behalf of an existing company, which was, and could only have been, the first defendant.'

■ Putting it all together

Answer guidelines

See the essay question at the start of the chapter.

Essay questions on pre-incorporation contracts are reasonably common and are very straightforward if you have a grasp of the key developments in the area. The crucial point to bear in mind is that the examiner is not just looking for a list of the various provisions, but also for some critical evaluation, in the form of some assessment of how well the current regime protects those involved. Also remember that pre-incorporation contracts represent another exception to the rule in *Salomon*.

Approaching the question

You should begin by explaining clearly what is meant by the term 'pre-incorporation contract' and spend a little time outlining why such contracts are legally flawed. This enables you to emphasise your wider understanding and will earn you marks. This should be followed by an explanation of how such contracts might arise, i.e. where the promoters of the company act in the mistaken belief that the company is already incorporated.

Important points to include

You should address the early treatment of such contracts under the common law, which is basically a consideration of *Kelner* v *Baxter* and *Newborne* v *Sensolid*, but it is not really sufficient merely to state the facts of the cases. You should also point out the unsatisfactory nature of looking to the way in which the document was signed in order to assess liability under the contract. This leads to a discussion of the current statutory provisions, originating in the First Company Law Directive and the European Communities Act 1972 and later the Companies Act 1985 and now the 2006 Act. Your discussion should also include *Phonogram* v *Lane* as an early example of the new regime in operation. Finally, offer some conclusion as to whether the increased certainty under the statutory regime outweighs the apparent unfairness to promoters who may find themselves personally liable on the contract. ▶

Make your answer stand out

- Emphasise the link between pre-incorporation contracts and the other 'lifting the veil' exceptions.

- Mention that this is an example of company law in England and Wales being influenced by EU law (in the form of the First Directive).

- Consider whether there is an argument for the company, rather than the promoters, to bear the burden of the contract as part of the broader encouragement of entrepreneurship.

READ TO IMPRESS

Bourne, N. (2002) 'Pre-incorporation contracts', 23 *Business Law Review* 110.

Griffiths, A. (1993) 'Agents without principles: pre-incorporation contracts and section 36C of the Companies Act 1985', 13(2) *Law Society Gazette* 241.

Hooley, R. (1991) 'Pre-incorporation contracts revisited', 50(3) *Cambridge Law Journal* 413.

Pennington, R. (2002) 'The validation of pre-incorporation contracts', 23 *Company Lawyer* 284.

Savirimuthu, J. (2003) 'Pre-incorporation contracts and the problem of corporate fundamentalism: are promoters proverbially profuse?', 24(7) *Company Lawyer* 196.

www.pearsoned.co.uk/lawexpress

 Go online to access more revision support including quizzes to test your knowledge, sample questions with answer guidelines, podcasts you can download, and more!

The constitution
of the company

5

■ Topic map

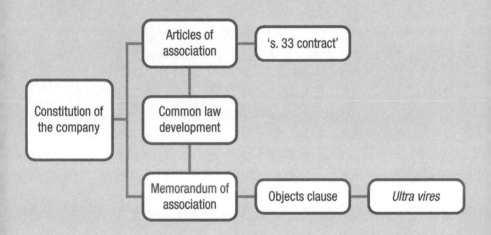

■ Introduction

Just as a country has a constitution, so does a company.

The concept of the company's 'constitution' sounds rather grand, but the principle is actually very simple. We are familiar with the idea that a country has a constitution (usually in the form of a single document) which acts as a rule book, setting out who has the power within the state and how they must use it in order to protect the citizens. In the same way, a company has people in power – the directors – who must be regulated in the way that they use their power in order to protect the citizens – the shareholders. As we will see, this is a slight simplification, but the general principle is much the same.

ASSESSMENT ADVICE

Historically, questions on the company's constitution itself have not been common. It is more usual to encounter questions on areas such as *ultra vires,* which require you to explain the doctrine as an example of how the constitution of the company operates to protect shareholders. However, as with almost every other area of company law, the Companies Act 2006 has made sweeping changes to the constitution of the company and, for this reason, it is quite possible that you may encounter a question which asks you to assess the impact of these changes.

■ Sample question

Could you answer this question? Below is a typical problem question that could arise on this topic. Guidelines on answering the question are included at the end of this chapter, whilst a sample essay question and guidance on tackling it can be found on the companion website.

PROBLEM QUESTION

'Thrill Ltd' is a company set up to run a small race track on an old disused airfield. The company stages 'track days' where the owners of high performance cars can race each other around the track. The company is run by two directors, Nathan and David, who each own 30 per cent of the company's shares. The remaining shares are owned by 10 other shareholders who each own 4 per cent of the shares but who take no part in the operation of the company.

▶

In order to increase income, Nathan and David begin to explore other means of exploiting the site and hit upon the idea of starting a gliding school. This will require an initial investment of £50,000 but they are confident that it will enhance the overall potential of the business. To this end, they approach a dealer to purchase a number of secondhand gliders. As they are the directors of the company, Nathan and David decide not to discuss the gliding venture with the other shareholders.

In August, Bernie, one of the other shareholders, learns of the plan and is alarmed by the proposal, particularly as a gliding school in a neighbouring town has recently gone into receivership after failing to generate sufficient business. He has examined the company's memorandum of association and has noticed that the company's objects are stated as 'the provision of motorsport facilities'. He wishes, if at all possible, to block the proposals but knows that Nathan and David are due to sign the contracts for the gliders within the next few days.

Advise Bernie.

Companies Act 2006

The 2006 Act has made a number of important changes in relation to the constitution of the company but it is crucial to remember that many of these changes will not automatically affect companies which are already registered with the 'old form' documentation under Companies Act (CA) 1985. For this reason, you must be aware of both.

The constitutional documents

The 'constitution' of the company comprises two key documents: the memorandum of association and the articles of association.

The memorandum of association

The memorandum is by far the shorter of the two documents and contains much less information than the articles. This is even more the case under Companies Act (CA) 2006, which transfers some material from the memorandum to the articles. The memorandum is often described as an 'external' document, i.e. it is aimed at third parties, such as potential customers and creditors, who might wish to know certain general information about the company.

Contents of the memorandum of association

CA 1985 (s. 2)	CA 2006
Name of the company	Statement that the promoters wish to form a company
Registered office (i.e. whether in England, Wales or Scotland)	Agreement to become members of the company and (in the case of a company with share capital) to take at least one share each
Objects clause (see below)	
Limitation of liability (i.e. whether or not the liability of members is limited)	
Share capital (i.e. the amount of the company's share capital and how it is divided)	
'Association clause' (stating that the promoters declare their intention to form the company and to take the number of shares attributed to them)	
[In addition, the memorandum of a public company must state that it is a public company – section 1(3)(a)]	

As you can see, the memorandum under CA 2006 is a very brief document, containing little real information. This reflects the intention of the Act to create a 'single constitutional document' for the company – the articles of association. This also extends to companies which are already incorporated.

KEY STATUTE

Companies Act 2006, section 28(1)

Provisions that immediately before the commencement of this Part were contained in a company's memorandum . . . are to be treated after the commencement of this Part as provisions of the company's articles.

Given the huge significance of the Companies Act 2006, the examiner will be impressed if you can show that you have read around the topic. A good source of background information on the Act can be found at the Department for Business, Innovation and Skills website: https://www.gov.uk/government/publications/companies-act-2006-executive-summary-of-evaluation-report

The objects clause

One provision of the 'old style' memorandum that has created some difficulty is the '**objects clause**', which states the type of business in which the company is meant to be engaged. Historically, this was highly significant as contracts made by the company for purposes not included in the objects clause could be deemed void under the doctrine of '*ultra vires*' (beyond powers). This was designed to protect shareholders by ensuring that their investment was used only for the company's stated purpose.

KEY DEFINITION: Objects clause

The clause within the company's constitution which states what is to be the purpose of the company.

KEY CASE

Ashbury Railway Carriage and Iron Company Ltd v *Riche* (1875) LR 7 HL 653 (HL)

Concerning: ultra vires

Facts

The appellant company's memorandum stated that the company's objects were 'To make, sell, or lend on hire . . . all kinds of railway plant . . . to carry on the business of mechanical engineers, and general contractors.' The directors entered into a contract with the respondent to employ him to construct a railway. The company later tried to avoid the contract, claiming that it had been *ultra vires*.

Legal principle

Held: the contract had been *ultra vires*, for the words 'general contractors' did not extend to the construction of an actual railway. Lord Selborne: 'The memorandum of association is under that Act their fundamental . . . unalterable law; and they are incorporated only for the objects and purposes expressed in that memorandum.'

KEY CASE

Re German Date Coffee Company (1882) 20 ChD 169 (CA)

Concerning: ultra vires

Facts

The objects clause of the company stated that it was formed to exploit a German patent which would be granted for making coffee from dates. However, the patents for the process were never granted so, instead, the company bought a Swedish patent for a similar process. This was challenged by some of the members of the company.

Legal principle

Held: because the German patent had not been granted, it was impossible to carry out the objects for which the company had been formed. Therefore, the actions of the company were *ultra vires*. Jessel MR: 'the whole substratum of the company is gone. Its business was not to make a substitute for coffee from dates, but to work a German patented invention in *Germany* . . . Therefore the shareholders have a right to say . . . "We did not enter into partnership on these terms".'

However, in order to avoid entering into *ultra vires* contracts, companies employed more and more complex objects clauses until it became almost impossible to hold that the directors had acted beyond their authority. Recognising this fact, a number of provisions were introduced by the Companies Act 1989 to amend the 1985 Act and reduce the significance of the objects clause.

KEY STATUTE

Companies Act 1985, section 3A

Statement of company's objects: general commercial company

Where the company's memorandum states that the object of the company is to carry on business as a general commercial company –

(a) the object of the company is to carry on any trade or business whatsoever, and

(b) the company has power to do all such things as are incidental or conducive to the carrying on of any trade or business by it.

Clearly an objects clause which permitted 'any trade or business whatsoever' made it extremely difficult to view an action as *ultra vires* and the 2006 Act has gone further by creating a presumption that the company's objects are unlimited unless the company expressly states otherwise.

KEY STATUTE

Companies Act 2006, section 31(1)

Statement of company's objects

(1) Unless a company's articles specifically restrict the objects of the company, its objects are unrestricted.

✎ EXAM TIP

Point out that section 31 refers to restrictions of the company's objects being expressed in the articles rather than the memorandum (where traditionally the objects clause was to be found). This is further indication of the shift away from the memorandum and towards the articles as the key source of information – the 'single constitutional document' envisaged under the 2006 Act.

KEY STATUTE

Companies Act 2006, section 40(1)

Power of directors to bind the company

(1) In favour of a person dealing with a company in good faith, the power of the directors to bind the company, or authorise others to do so, is deemed to be free of any limitation under the company's constitution.

Therefore, under section 40, it is almost impossible to challenge a contract with a third party on the basis that it conflicts with the objects clause. This might be seen as abolishing the doctrine of *ultra vires* but there remains the possibility of a challenge by a shareholder.

KEY STATUTE

Companies Act 2006, section 40(4)

Power of directors to bind the company

(4) This section does not affect any right of a member of the company to bring proceedings to restrain the doing of an action that is beyond the powers of the directors. But no such proceedings lie in respect of an act to be done in fulfilment of a legal obligation arising from a previous act of the company.

In this way, a shareholder can apply to the court to prevent the company from entering into a contract which would otherwise be *ultra vires* but, crucially, this does not apply if the contract has been agreed and the company is acting 'in fulfilment of a legal obligation'.

■ The articles of association

The second document which forms part of the constitution of the company is the articles of association. This is a much more complex document and, unlike the memorandum, is essentially an *internal* document as it contains the detailed rules governing important aspects of the company's organisation. These include:

- shares (their issue and the rights attached to them, dividends, etc.);
- the conduct of company meetings;
- the role and powers of directors.

The articles contain the detailed rules which govern the conduct of directors, the rights of shareholders and the relationship between the two.

Model Articles

The pro-forma articles of association which are available for companies to adopt are known as 'the Model Articles' and run to over fifty 'Articles' (equivalent to section numbers). The articles of association were previously known as 'Table A' and you may continue to see references to these in companies which were registered under the old regime.

 EXAM TIP

Although the Model Articles is a complex document, your understanding of its impact will be assisted if you are at least familiar with its style and layout. The latest version can be found at www.companieshouse.gov.uk/about/modelArticles/modelArticles.shtml

✓ **Make your answer stand out**

The shift from memorandum and articles towards a 'single constitutional document' is one of the key structural implications of the 2006 Act. The statute was the result of years of research and consultation and the examiner will be impressed by any reference which shows that you are aware of the debates leading up to the passage of the Act. For some discussion of various aspects of the reforms, see Arora (2003).

The articles as terms of a contract

The articles regulate the relationship between the shareholders and the company and confer enforceable rights on members. This is expressed by means of contractual terms, with the Act treating the articles of association as the terms of a contract between the company and its members.

KEY STATUTE

Companies Act 2006, section 33(1)

Effect of company's constitution

(1) The provisions of a company's constitution bind the company and its members to the same extent as if there were covenants on the part of the company and of each member to observe those provisions.

❗ Don't be tempted to . . .

This provision replaces section 14 of the Companies Act 1985, which created what is frequently referred to as the 's. 14 contract'. Remember that this is the same provision and creates the same rights and obligations.

KEY CASE

Hickman v *Kent or Romney Marsh Sheepbreeders' Association* (1920) 37 TLR 163 (CA)

Concerning: the articles as a contract

Facts

The claimant became a member of the defendant association and agreed to abide by its rules and regulations. Under the articles of association, any dispute between a member and the association had to be referred to arbitration before any litigation could be contemplated. The claimant ignored this and brought a court action against the association. The defendants applied for a stay of the action in order to refer the dispute to arbitration in accordance with the articles.

Legal principle

Held: the articles must be treated as a statutory agreement between the members and the association. Therefore, the member had to abide by the provision.

KEY CASE

Rayfield v *Hands* [1960] Ch 1 (PD and Admlty)

Concerning: articles as a contract

Facts

Under the company's articles, any member wishing to sell their shares had to approach the directors who were required to 'take the said shares equally between them at a fair value'. The claimant did so but the directors refused to buy his shares.

Legal principle

Held: the articles constituted the terms of a contract between the company and the members. Therefore, the directors had no choice but to buy the shares. Vaisey J: 'Not one of the judges in the case to which I have already referred . . . showed any . . . surprise in the assumption . . . of a contract between directors being formed by the terms of a company's articles. I . . . find in this case a contract similarly formed between a member and member-directors in relation to their holdings of the company's shares in its articles.'

However, the provision only applies to rights and obligations which arise by means of the contract of membership (i.e. the contract for purchase of shares). Therefore, members cannot use this section to enforce rights under another contract simply because they are members of the company.

KEY CASE

Beattie v *E & F Beattie Ltd* [1938] Ch 708 (CA)

Concerning: non-enforceable contractual terms

Facts

The claimant was a director and shareholder in the company and brought an action against another director alleging that he had made certain payments to himself which were in excess of his salary. The articles contained an arbitration clause (as in *Hickman* above) and the defendant sought to hold the claimant to the terms of the articles.

Legal principle

Held: the disputed matter arose, not under the contract for the sale of shares in the company but under the director's contract of employment. This was an entirely different contract and so was not subject to the arbitration clause in the articles. Greene MR: 'the two rights are, in my judgement, perfectly distinct and quite different – the general right of a member as a member and the right which the appellant as a party to the dispute is seeking to enforce.'

Alteration of the articles

Under CA 2006, section 21 a company can alter its articles by special resolution (75 per cent of votes cast). There are, however, a number of restrictions on the changes that can be made. Most obviously, the company cannot make changes which contravene either company law or an order of the court. Beyond this, any change must be '*bona fide* for the benefit of the company as a whole'.

KEY CASE

Allen v *Gold Reefs of West Africa Ltd* [1900] 1 Ch 656 (CA)

Concerning: alteration to the articles of association

Facts

The company, by way of purchase money for the property acquired by it, allotted fully paid shares to Z who also had allotted to him shares which were not paid up. At his death he owed money to the company for the unpaid shares, but his assets were insufficient to pay the arrears. The company altered the articles to create a right over Z's fully paid shares.

Legal principle

Held: in approving the company's power to make the alteration to the articles, Lindley MR: 'The power thus conferred on companies to alter the regulations contained in their articles is limited only by the provisions contained in the statute and the conditions contained in the company's memorandum of association . . . however . . . the power conferred by it must, like all other powers, be exercised subject to those general principles of law and equity which are applicable to all powers conferred on majorities and enabling them to bind minorities. It must be exercised, not only in the manner required by law, but also *bona fide* for the benefit of the company as a whole.'

On this basis, although not commonplace, the courts may overturn an alteration if it is held not to satisfy the '*bona fide*' test.

KEY CASE

Brown v *British Abrasive Wheel Co. Ltd* [1919] 1 Ch 290 (Ch)

Concerning: alteration to the articles of association

Facts

The company desperately needed additional capital and the majority shareholders (who held 98 per cent of the shares in the company) were willing to provide this capital, but only if they could buy the remaining shares in the company. Having failed to agree this with the minority shareholders, they proposed to pass an article enabling them to purchase the minority shares compulsorily

Legal principle

Held: Astbury J: 'The defendants contend that it is for the benefit of the company as a whole because in default of further capital the company might have to go into liquidation . . . [but] . . . the proposed alteration is not directly concerned with the provision of further capital, nor does it insure that it will be provided. It is merely for the benefit of the majority.'

Another situation which has caused concern is the possibility of a company seeking to 'entrench' provisions within the articles – i.e. to make them incapable of later alteration. Historically, this has been prohibited under company law.

Walker v *London Tramways Co.* **(1879) 12 Ch D 705 (Ch)**
Concerning: alteration to the articles of association

Facts

The articles of association provided that the company could set apart 1 per cent of the paid-up capital as a 'contingencies fund' and that this provision could not be changed. The directors wished to use the contingencies fund to pay for repairs to the tramway (which by a former order of the court they were precluded from doing) and so submitted a resolution to alter the articles for this purpose.

Legal principle

Held: the company could not contract out of section 50 of the Companies Act 1862 which allowed a company to alter any of the articles of association.

However, the Companies Act 2006 now provides for a limited degree of entrenchment.

KEY STATUTE

Companies Act 2006, section 22

22 Entrenched provisions of the articles

(1) A company's articles may contain provision ('provision for entrenchment') to the effect that specified provisions of the articles may be amended or repealed only if conditions are met, or procedures are complied with, that are more restrictive than those applicable in the case of a special resolution.

(2) Provision for entrenchment may only be made –

    (a) in the company's articles on formation, or

    (b) by an amendment of the company's articles agreed to by all the members of the company.

(3) Provision for entrenchment does not prevent amendment of the company's articles –

    (a) by agreement of all the members of the company, or

    (b) by order of a court or other authority having power to alter the company's articles.

(4) Nothing in this section affects any power of a court or other authority to alter a company's articles.

Note, however, that this does not mean that companies can draft provisions in the articles that can *never* be changed, only that some provisions may be made more difficult to alter.

■ Putting it all together

Answer guidelines

See the problem question at the start of the chapter.

Approaching the question

Issues such as interpretation of the objects clause and *ultra vires* lend themselves easily to problem questions and this is a typical example. This is an area of company law where there has been considerable revision over the years and the examiner will expect you to place the various changes within their proper context. Although the combined effect of the changes introduced by the Companies Act 1985, Companies Act 1989 and Companies Act 2006 has greatly reduced the significance of the objects clause, there remains the possibility of a successful challenge to the actions of directors and the examiner will want to see that you can recognise the circumstances where this might arise.

Important points to include

You should begin by explaining clearly the significance of the objects clause as a restriction on the directors, requiring them to utilise the shareholders' investment for the agreed purpose. This requires you to outline the doctrine of *ultra vires* and this is a good opportunity to include some of the early case law to emphasise your knowledge. In this scenario, it is clear that the intended conduct (the gliding school) is outside the objects clause of the company and so you need to assess whether an action to restrain the directors is possible. You should list the various provisions which have undermined the doctrine of *ultra vires* and which make it virtually impossible for a third party to challenge a company contract on these grounds. However, we can see that the challenge in this case comes from a shareholder and so there remains the possibility of a challenge under CA 2006, section 40(4). The key point to make here is that such a challenge can only succeed where the contract has not actually been agreed (which is the case here), so Bernie could mount a challenge.

Make your answer stand out

- Include reference to the wider debate on the use of the objects clause and the weakening of the doctrine of *ultra vires* to emphasise your knowledge.

- Make the point that the company could redraft its objects clause to adopt the 'general commercial company' model of CA 1985, section 3A.

- Include reference to the most recent changes in CA 2006 and the adoption of the 'single constitutional document' which sees the objects clause move from the memorandum to the articles of association, and the effect of section 31 which does not require the company even to have an objects clause unless it wishes to do so.

READ TO IMPRESS

Arora, A. (2003) 'Reforming the Company Acts', 5(6) *Finance and Credit Law* 1.

Pike, A. (2008) 'Articles of association and CA 2006', 31(26) *Company Secretary's Review* 201.

Ryan, C. (2008) 'The statutory contract under section 33 of the Companies Act 2006: the legal consequences for banks Pt I', 6 *Journal of International Banking and Finance Law* 304.

Ryan, C. (2008) 'The statutory contract under section 33 of the Companies Act 2006: the legal consequences for banks Pt II', 7 *Journal of International Banking and Finance Law* 360.

www.pearsoned.co.uk/lawexpress

 Go online to access more revision support including quizzes to test your knowledge, sample questions with answer guidelines, podcasts you can download, and more!

Directors

Revision checklist

Essential points you should know:

- [ ] The management role of directors within the company and their relationship with shareholders
- [ ] The procedures for appointment and removal of directors
- [ ] The fiduciary duties which apply to directors in the performance of their duties
- [ ] The impact of CA 2006 and the introduction of statutory directors' duties

■ Topic map

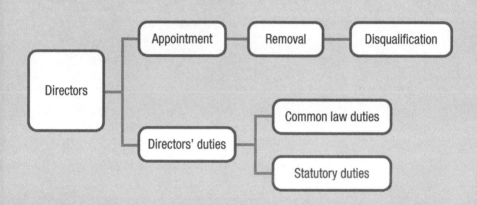

■ Introduction

The directors manage the company on behalf of the members. They determine whether the company succeeds or fails.

The members of the company may provide the financial investment which allows the company to exist, but they are seldom in a position to exercise day-to-day control over how the company operates. For this reason, they need the directors to manage the company and take the day-to-day decisions necessary to maximise the company's profits. This places the directors in a position of considerable power, with the authority to decide which direction the company will take. They also have access to valuable and confidential information which others, including the members, do not have and this raises the prospect of a conflict between their responsibility to the company and their own interests. Consequently, directors are subject to a series of duties which students of company law must understand.

ASSESSMENT ADVICE

Traditionally, directors' duties have been the most frequently examined aspect of this topic and this is likely to continue, particularly following the introduction of statutory directors' duties under CA 2006.

Essay questions

Essay questions may require you to chart the development of the common law directors' duties before moving on to consider application of the statutory duties. This type of question requires a thorough knowledge of both the common law rules and the various duties introduced by CA 2006.

Problem questions

Problem questions will pose a scenario which suggests a breach of directors' duties. This may relate to a possible conflict of interest or misuse of directors' powers. As with essay questions, although the emphasis is now on the statutory duties under CA 2006, a strong answer will also include reference to the old common law duties.

■ Sample question

Could you answer this question? Below is a typical problem question that could arise on this topic. Guidelines on answering the question are included at the end of this chapter, whilst a sample essay question and guidance on tackling it can be found on the companion website.

Omar, Charlie and Karen are the directors and sole shareholders of 'Communisolutions Ltd', a company involved in the supply and installation of networked IT systems for hospitals, local authorities and other large organisations. The company was incorporated in 1998 with Omar holding 20 per cent of the shares and Charlie and Karen holding 40 per cent each.

Charlie is the technical director of the company and part of his role is to deal with prospective customers. In this role, he negotiates the following contracts:

(a) With Finisham Maternity Hospital for the installation of a computerised patient record system. Part of the contract entails the supply of custom-built computer desks. Charlie informs Omar and Karen that he has arranged to purchase these at a favourable price from 'PC Comfort Ltd'. He neglects to tell them that 'PC Comfort Ltd' is run by his brother Peter and that Peter has agreed to 'see him right' when the contract is fulfilled.

(b) With the local medical centre for the installation of a computerised appointments and call-out system for the doctors and district nurses. As this is a relatively small contract, Charlie decides not to tell Omar and Karen about it. He supplies and installs the system himself, with some assistance from Peter, with whom he splits the profit.

Discuss.

Directors

KEY STATUTE

Companies Act 2006, section 250

'Director'

In the Companies Acts 'director' includes any person occupying the position of director, by whatever name called.

In this way, the definition of 'director' is broad but clearly relates to an individual with direct control over the day-to-day management of the company. For this reason, the term 'director' can, on occasion, also extend to '*de facto*' directors (persons who act in the role of director without ever having been formally appointed as such) and 'shadow' directors (persons on whose directions or instructions the company is accustomed to act).

KEY CASE

Gemma Ltd v *Davies* [2008] EWHC 546 (Ch)

Concerning: defining a 'de facto' *or 'shadow' director*

Facts

G was the director of a building business and his wife was the company secretary. As part of a claim against the company the court was required to consider whether liability should be extended to the wife as a *de facto* director of the company.

Legal principle

Held: the tests to be applied in deciding whether a person was a shadow or *de facto* director were whether they undertook functions in relation to the company which could properly be discharged only by a director, whether they participated in directing the affairs of the company on an equal footing and not in a subordinate role, and whether they assumed the status and functions of a company director, exercising real influence in the corporate governance of the company. This was not the case in relation to the wife. Gaunt J: '[Hers] was a purely clerical task involving no decision-making at all.'

KEY CASE

Re Paycheck Services 3 Ltd; Revenue & Customs Commissioners and another v *Holland* [2010] UKSC 51 (SC)

Concerning: defining a 'de facto' *or 'shadow' director*

Facts

H and his wife set up a complicated structure of composite companies to administer the business and tax affairs of contractors working in various sectors. H was not officially the director of any of the composite companies. The sole director of each company was another company (the corporate director) of which he was director. This complex structure was designed to avoid the true liability for corporation tax. When the companies went into liquidation, HMRC sought to recover the outstanding tax, alleging that, as *de facto* directors of the companies, H and his wife had been guilty of misfeasance and breaches of duty.

Legal principle

Held (by a majority of 3 to 2): H had not acted as a *de facto* director of the composite companies. The fact that he had been a director of the corporate director was not sufficient to establish that he was part of the corporate governance of the composite companies or that he assumed fiduciary duties in respect of them. Lord Hope: 'It has not been shown that Mr Holland was acting as *de facto* director of the composite companies so as to make him responsible for the misuse of their assets.'

Make your answer stand out

The role and responsibilities of directors have provoked a great deal of discussion over recent years, with a number of reports and codes of conduct aimed at regulating the management of companies. Any reading which you can undertake around this subject will lend your answers greater depth and enhance your overall mark. For an account of some of the key developments and debates, see Drew (1995), Chambers (2003) and Spedding (2004).

■ Appointment of directors

Under CA 2006, section 154 a private limited company must have at least one director, and a public limited company must have at least two. Section 162 also requires the company to maintain a register of directors. The procedure for appointment of directors is usually contained in the articles of association, which provide for appointment by the members of the company.

KEY STATUTORY PROVISION

Model Articles

17. – (1) Any person who is willing to act as a director, and is permitted by law to do so, may be appointed to be a director –

   (a) by ordinary resolution, or

   (b) by a decision of the directors.

Removal

Directors can be removed at any time by ordinary resolution (simple majority of votes cast) under CA 2006, section 168.

✎ EXAM TIP

When discussing the removal of directors make a point of mentioning that the use of an ordinary resolution, rather than a special resolution, to remove a director makes the position of directors deliberately precarious. In this way, they must make every effort to ensure the company's success or face removal.

Who can be a director?

There are a number of restrictions under both CA 2006 and the Company Directors Disqualification Act 1986 (CDDA 1986) regulating who can act as a director of a limited company. These include the following:

Persons aged under 16

Under CA 2006, section 157 a person under 16 years of age cannot act as a company director. Note that the Act also removed the restriction on persons over 70 years of age acting as a director by repealing section 293 of CA 1985.

Bankrupts

Under CDDA 1986, an undischarged bankrupt cannot act as a director without leave from the court.

Disqualified persons

CDDA 1986 provides for a person to be disqualified from acting as a director of a company for a specified period. If a person ignores such a disqualification order, they commit a criminal offence under section 13 of the Act and are liable to imprisonment and/or fine. They also lose the protection of limited liability and are personally liable for the debts of the company. The Act provides for the court to make a discretionary disqualification order on certain grounds but there is also mandatory disqualification for general unfitness.

Discretionary disqualification under CDDA 1986

Ground for disqualification	Maximum period of disqualification
Conviction of an indictable offence relating to the 'promotion, formation or management' of a company (CDDA 1986, s. 2)	15 years
Persistent default of companies legislation relating to the filing of documents with the Registrar of Companies (CDDA 1986, s. 3)	5 years
Fraudulent activity in the winding up of a company (CDDA 1986, s. 4)	15 years
Participation in 'wrongful trading' (CDDA 1986, s. 10)	15 years

Mandatory disqualification under CDDA 1986

Company Directors Disqualification Act 1986, section 6(1)

Duty of court to disqualify unfit directors of insolvent companies

(1) The court shall make a disqualification order against a person in any case where, on an application under this section, it is satisfied –

    (a) that he is or has been a director of a company which has at any time become insolvent (whether while he was a director or subsequently), and

    (b) that his conduct as a director of that company (either taken alone or taken together with his conduct as a director of any other company or companies) makes him unfit to be concerned in the management of a company.

Under section 6 the disqualification must be for a minimum of 2 years and can be up to a maximum of 15 years. What precisely evidences 'unfitness' will depend on the circumstances of the case.

■ Directors' duties

One of the most important (and most frequently examined) aspects of the law affecting directors is the various duties which are imposed on those managing companies.

Directors are said to owe a 'fiduciary' duty to the company. That is a duty which is based on trust and so, to some degree, this resembles the duty owed by doctors to their patients and by lawyers to their clients.

Directors' duties are likely to continue as a popular exam topic in light of the changes contained in CA 2006, which introduced statutory directors' duties to replace the old common law rules. However, you will still need to understand the old rules for two reasons: first, an exam question may ask you to chart the development of directors' duties from the common law to the statutory rules; secondly, the Act expressly states that the old common law rules are to be used to assist interpretation of the new statutory provisions.

Companies Act 2006, section 170(4)

Scope and nature of general duties

(4) The general duties [under the 2006 Act] shall be interpreted and applied in the same way as common law rules or equitable principles, and regard shall be had to the corresponding common law rules and equitable principles in interpreting and applying the general duties.

Directors' duties under CA 2006

As stated above, the key duties imposed on directors of companies are now governed by CA 2006. These are as follows:

Section	Duty
s. 171	Duty to act within powers (i.e. to act within the constitution of the company and to use powers only for the purpose for which they were given)
s. 172	Duty to promote the success of the company (see below)
s. 173	Duty to exercise independent judgement
s. 174	Duty to exercise reasonable care, skill and diligence (i.e. that which may be reasonably expected of a person carrying out the function of director and with the knowledge, skill and experience of this particular director)
s. 175	Duty to avoid conflict of interest (unless this has been authorised by the company)
s. 176	Duty not to accept benefits from third parties
s. 177	Duty to declare interests in proposed transactions with the company

Section 171 – Duty to act within powers

KEY STATUTE

Companies Act 2006, section 171

Duty to act within powers

A director of a company must –

(a) act in accordance with the company's constitution, and

(b) only exercise powers for the purposes for which they are conferred.

As can be seen, there are two distinct elements to this duty: first, to act within the limits imposed by the company's constitution and, secondly, to exercise powers for the intended purpose. The first requirement, to act within the constitution of the company, is of lesser significance following the abolition of the requirement for a company to have an objects clause but there may remain some restrictions on the powers of the director imposed by the articles of association.

The second requirement of section 171, to exercise powers only for the purposes for which they are conferred, largely restates the previous common law duty to act for a 'proper purpose'. This has previously arisen most frequently in relation to the exercise of powers such as the issuing of shares.

Hogg v *Cramphorn* [1967] Ch 254 (Ch)

Concerning: actions for an improper purpose

Facts

In order to prevent a takeover bid for the company, the directors arranged for an interest-free loan to the company's pension fund so that the fund could purchase shares in the company. The new shares would have special voting rights and were being issued subject to an agreement that the votes would be cast to oppose the takeover bid. A minority shareholder objected even though the directors genuinely thought that the takeover would damage the company.

Legal principle

Held: Buckley J: 'It is common ground that the directors were not actuated by any unworthy motives of personal advantage, but acted as they did in an honest belief that they were doing what was for the good of the company. [However] the power to issue shares was a fiduciary power and if, as I think, it was exercised for an improper motive, the issue of these shares is liable to be set aside.'

Section 172 – Duty to promote the success of the company

Perhaps the most far-reaching of the new duties is under section 172 which imposes a wide-ranging obligation on directors to consider various factors in the running of the business.

Companies Act 2006, section 172(1)

Duty to promote the success of the company

(1) A director of a company must act in the way he considers, in good faith, would be most likely to promote the success of the company for the benefit of its members as a whole, and in doing so have regard (amongst other matters) to –

   (a) the likely consequences of any decision in the long term,

   (b) the interests of the company's employees,

   (c) the need to foster the company's business relationships with suppliers, customers and others,

   (d) the impact of the company's operations on the community and the environment,

   (e) the desirability of the company maintaining a reputation for high standards of business conduct, and

   (f) the need to act fairly as between members of the company.

As with the other statutory duties, section 172 embodies some of the principles previously expressed in the common law duties. This provision restates the previous fiduciary duty to act '*bona fide*' or 'in good faith' in the interests of the company.

KEY CASE

Re Smith and Fawcett Ltd [1942] Ch 304 (CA)

Concerning: the duty to act bona fide

Facts

The articles of the company allowed the directors discretion to refuse to register any transfer of company shares. All of the company's shares were owned by two directors but, when one died, the other refused to register the transfer of the deceased's shareholding to his son, offering instead to buy the shares from him.

Legal principle

Held: such fiduciary powers must be exercised in the interests of the company and there was nothing to show that they had been misused in this case. Lord Greene MR: 'The principles to be applied . . . are, for the present purposes, free from doubt. [Directors] must exercise their discretion *bona fide* in what they consider – not what a court may consider – is in the interests of the company.'

Note the subjective nature of the duty. Providing the actions are in good faith, it is what the director considers to be in the best interests of the company, rather than what the court might see as appropriate. This emphasis is reflected in the wording of section 172(1).

KEY CASE

Regentcrest plc (in liquidation) v *Cohen and another* [2000] All ER (D) 747 (Ch)

Concerning: the duty to act bona fide

Facts

The facts of this case are lengthy and complicated and to summarise them here would add little to an understanding of the legal principle outlined below. Remember that examiners are usually looking for an understanding of the *ratio* and legal principle and that reciting the facts in an exam will not improve your grade.

Legal principle

Held: the duty imposed on directors to act *bona fide* in the interests of the company was a subjective one and the question to be determined was whether the director honestly believed that his actions were in the best interests of the company. Parker J: 'The question is not whether, viewed objectively by the court, the particular act or omission . . . was in fact in the interests of the company . . . Rather, the question is whether the director honestly believed that his act or omission was in the interests of the company.'

Section 173 – Duty to exercise independent judgement

KEY STATUTE

Companies Act 2006, section 173

Duty to exercise independent judgement

(1) A director of a company must exercise independent judgment.

(2) This duty is not infringed by his acting –

 (a) in accordance with an agreement duly entered into by the company that restricts the future exercise of discretion by its directors, or

 (b) in a way authorised by the company's constitution.

This provision acts to prevent directors from restricting the future operation of their discretion to exercise their judgement to act in the interests of the company.

KEY CASE

Boulting and another v *Association of Cinematograph Television and Allied Technicians* **[1963] 1 All ER 716 (CA)**

Concerning: the duty to exercise independent judgement

Facts

The managing directors of a film production company faced demands from the union representing technical staff employed within the industry that they join the union or face industrial action. The directors argued that to be members of the same union as their workers would create a conflict of interest.

Legal principle

Held: the directors were eligible for union membership but, in his dissenting judgment, Lord Denning stated: 'It seems to me that no one, who has duties of a fiduciary nature to discharge, can be allowed to enter into an engagement by which he binds himself to disregard those duties or to act inconsistently with them. No stipulation is lawful by which he agrees to carry out his duties in accordance with the instructions of another rather than on his own conscientious judgment; or by which he agrees to subordinate the interests of those whom he must protect to the interests of someone else.'

Section 174 – Duty to exercise reasonable care, skill and diligence

KEY STATUTE

Companies Act 2006, section 174

Duty to exercise reasonable care, skill and diligence

(1) A director of a company must exercise reasonable care, skill and diligence.

(2) This means the care, skill and diligence that would be exercised by a reasonably diligent person with –

    (a) the general knowledge, skill and experience that may reasonably be expected of a person carrying out the functions carried out by the director in relation to the company, and

    (b) the general knowledge, skill and experience that the director has.

This provision restates the duty of 'care and skill' imposed on directors under the common law.

KEY CASE

Dorchester Finance Co. Ltd v *Stebbing* **[1989] BCLC 498 (Ch)**

Concerning: the duty of care and skill

Facts

Although the company had three directors, most of the duties were undertaken by S. The others took little interest in the management of the company, seldom visited the offices and signed blank cheques for S to complete. S misappropriated company funds and all three directors faced a claim for negligence.

Legal principle

Held: a director was required to perform his duties with the skill which could be reasonably expected from a person with his knowledge and experience and to take such care as an ordinary man might be expected to take on his own behalf, acting in good faith and in the interests of the company. Foster J: 'The signing of blank cheques [by the other directors] was in my judgment negligent, as it allowed Stebbing to do as he pleased. Apart from that they not only failed to exhibit the necessary skill and care in the performance of their duties as directors, but also failed to perform any duty at all as directors of Dorchester.'

Section 175 – Duty to avoid conflicts of interest

KEY STATUTE

Companies Act 2006, section 175

Duty to avoid conflicts of interest

(1) A director of a company must avoid a situation in which he has, or can have, a direct or indirect interest that conflicts, or possibly may conflict, with the interests of the company.

(2) This applies in particular to the exploitation of any property, information or opportunity (and it is immaterial whether the company could take advantage of the property, information or opportunity).

(3) This duty does not apply to a conflict of interest arising in relation to a transaction or arrangement with the company.

(4) This duty is not infringed –

    (a) if the situation cannot reasonably be regarded as likely to give rise to a conflict of interest; or

    (b) if the matter has been authorised by the directors.

(5) Authorisation may be given by the directors –

    (a) where the company is a private company and nothing in the company's constitution invalidates such authorisation, by the matter being proposed to and authorised by the directors; or

    (b) where the company is a public company and its constitution includes provision enabling the directors to authorise the matter, by the matter being proposed to and authorised by them in accordance with the constitution.

(6) The authorisation is effective only if –

    (a) any requirement as to the quorum at the meeting at which the matter is considered is met without counting the director in question or any other interested director, and

    (b) the matter was agreed to without their voting or would have been agreed to if their votes had not been counted.

(7) Any reference in this section to a conflict of interest includes a conflict of interest and duty and a conflict of duties.

This provision addresses two principles known as the 'no conflict' rule and the 'no profit' rule. As such this is aimed at those situations where an individual has a conflict of interest with the company of which they are director. Under the common law, many of these cases were described in terms of the 'corporate opportunity doctrine' which gave the company an equitable claim over any profit made by the director where the opportunity had arisen as a result of their directorship of the company.

KEY CASE

Industrial Development Consultants Ltd v *Cooley* [1972] 2 All ER 162 (Assizes)
Concerning: corporate opportunity doctrine

Facts

The defendant was a director of a company which he left in order to take up a valuable contract for himself which could have gone to the company.

Legal principle

Held: the defendant had embarked on a deliberate course of conduct which had put his personal interests in direct conflict with his duty as a director of the company. He was, therefore, in breach of his fiduciary duty. Roskill J: 'an order for an account will be issued because the defendant made and will make his profit as a result of having allowed his interests and his duty to conflict.'

KEY CASE

CMS Dolphin Ltd v *Simonet and another* [2001] All ER (D) 294 (May) (Ch)
Concerning: maturing business opportunity

Facts

A director of a marketing company left his post to set up a competing business to which he transferred many of the first company's clients and much of its business.

Legal principle

Held: although there was nothing to prevent a director from resigning and setting up another business, here the defendant had utilised information gained as a result of his original directorship and had deprived the company of 'maturing business opportunities'. This constituted a breach of his fiduciary duty. Collins J: 'the underlying basis of the liability of a director who exploits after his resignation a maturing business opportunity of the company is that the opportunity is to be treated as if it were property of the company in relation to which the director had fiduciary duties.'

6 DIRECTORS

KEY CASE

Island Export Finance Ltd v *Umunna and another* [1986] BCLC 460 (QBD)

Concerning: maturing business opportunity

Facts

U was the managing director of IEF Ltd and secured a contract for the company to supply post boxes to Cameroon. After the completion of the contract, U resigned from the company and, some time later, obtained another contract from the Cameroon authorities. IEF sued for the profit which he had made.

Legal principle

Held: U was not required to repay the money as he had not deprived his former company of a 'maturing business opportunity'. IEF had not been actively pursuing such an opportunity and U had not resigned in order to pursue such an opportunity. Therefore, there had been no breach of fiduciary duty. Hutchison J: 'The knowledge of a potential market which could be exploited . . . was necessarily something which had become part of Mr Umunna's own skill and knowledge and, as such, something which the law allowed him to use for his own benefit and in competition with the plaintiff after cessation of his appointment.'

In the application of section 175 there is the potential for overlap with the last two statutory duties.

KEY STATUTE

Companies Act 2006, section 176

Duty not to accept benefits from third parties

(1) A director of a company must not accept a benefit from a third party conferred by reason of –

(a) his being a director, or

(b) his doing (or not doing) anything as director.

(2) A 'third party' means a person other than the company, an associated body corporate or a person acting on behalf of the company or an associated body corporate.

(3) Benefits received by a director from a person by whom his services (as a director or otherwise) are provided to the company are not regarded as conferred by a third party.

(4) This duty is not infringed if the acceptance of the benefit cannot reasonably be regarded as likely to give rise to a conflict of interest.

(5) Any reference in this section to a conflict of interest includes a conflict of interest and duty and a conflict of duties.

Companies Act 2006, section 177

Duty to declare interest in proposed transaction or arrangement

(1) If a director of a company is in any way, directly or indirectly, interested in a proposed transaction or arrangement with the company, he must declare the nature and extent of that interest to the other directors.

(2) The declaration may (but need not) be made –

   (a) at a meeting of the directors, or

   (b) by notice to the directors in accordance with –

      (i) section 184 (notice in writing), or

      (ii) section 185 (general notice).

(3) If a declaration of interest under this section proves to be, or becomes, inaccurate or incomplete, a further declaration must be made.

(4) Any declaration required by this section must be made before the company enters into the transaction or arrangement.

(5) This section does not require a declaration of an interest of which the director is not aware or where the director is not aware of the transaction or arrangement in question.

   For this purpose a director is treated as being aware of matters of which he ought reasonably to be aware.

(6) A director need not declare an interest –

   (a) if it cannot reasonably be regarded as likely to give rise to a conflict of interest;

   (b) if, or to the extent that, the other directors are already aware of it (and for this purpose the other directors are treated as aware of anything of which they ought reasonably to be aware); or

   (c) if, or to the extent that, it concerns terms of his service contract that have been or are to be considered –

      (i) by a meeting of the directors, or

      (ii) by a committee of the directors appointed for the purpose under the company's constitution.

Looking at the two provisions, it can be seen that, although there may appear to be a degree of similarity, they are aimed at slightly different situations. Section 176 addresses the prospect of a director taking a benefit, which should be interpreted broadly, from a third party, whereas section 177 applies where the director has an interest in a transaction with the company itself.

KEY CASE

Boston Deep Sea Fishing & Ice Co. v *Ansell* (1888) 39 Ch D 339 (CA)

Concerning: secret profit

Facts

The defendant was a director of the company and was authorised to purchase some ships for the company. Unknown to the other directors, he took a secret commission from the shipbuilders to award them the contract.

Legal principle

Head: as the director had only been able to obtain the commission because he was a director he was liable to repay the commission to the company. Bowen LJ: 'It is not that the money ought to have gone into the principal's hands in the first instance. It is because it is contrary to equity that the agent or the servant should retain money so received without the knowledge of his master.'

Make your answer stand out

The examiner will give you credit for a more in-depth knowledge of both the duties and the debate which surrounded their introduction. See Davidson (2007) and Chuah (2007).

REVISION NOTE

Remember that the topic of directors' duties under CA 2006 should be revised in conjunction with derivative actions (see Chapter 8).

Make your answer stand out

It should be noted that requiring directors to consider issues such as their employees and the environment is a new development in UK company law and the broad nature of the duty imposed by section 172 has prompted debate surrounding what has been termed 'enlightened shareholder value'. For a discussion of the topic, see Beale (2007).

■ Putting it all together

Answer guidelines

See the problem question at the start of the chapter.

Approaching the question

Directors' duties have always been a popular exam topic and this is a typical example of a problem question on the subject. As you can see, this question concentrates on 'conflict of interest' and the director who makes a secret profit at the expense of the company. Following the introduction of CA 2006, such questions will require both an account of the key common law authorities and also the relevant provisions of the Act. Remember, however, that the Act expressly provides that the new statutory duties are to be interpreted in the same way as the old common law rules and so those authorities remain important.

Important points to include

You should begin by providing a general introduction to the subject of directors' duties, emphasising the fiduciary nature of such duties and the imbalance of power and knowledge between shareholders and directors which makes such obligations necessary. Although the question concentrates on conflict of interest situations, you should also briefly outline the other common law duties, such as care and skill, proper purpose, *bona fide*, etc. to emphasise your understanding of the topic and you should also emphasise that CA 2006 has replaced the common law duties with statutory obligations.

Moving on to the scenario, we can see that the first example involves Charlie accepting a secret payment from the supplier company. This raises the possible application of section 175, section 176 and section 177 with the facts of the case resembling those of *Boston Deep Sea Fishing* v *Ansell*. In this case the director was ordered to repay the profit to the company and this is the likely outcome in our scenario. In the second example, Charlie takes the opportunity entirely and so the facts are more reminiscent of *Industrial Development Consultants Ltd* v *Cooley* where, once again, the director was ordered to repay the money earned. In addressing the question it is important to make the distinction between the first example (where the company does complete the contract but the director makes a secret profit) and the second (where the director takes the contract entirely for himself and the company gets nothing). In both cases, there has been a breach of duty.

▶

Make your answer stand out

- Emphasise the concept of depriving the company of a 'maturing business opportunity' as the basis for the conflict of interest.

- Be sure to state that the common law rules are now replaced by the statutory provisions but still have relevance as aids to construction.

- You can also point out that the courts have viewed directors in such cases as holding their profit 'on trust' for the company. This provides the theoretical justification for the company demanding repayment of the money earned.

READ TO IMPRESS

Beale, P. (2007) 'Directors beware?', 157 *New Law Journal* 1033.

Chambers, A. (2003) 'The revised combined code', 27(11) *Company Secretary's Review* 81.

Chuah, J. (2007) 'The new Companies Act 2006 and directors' duties', 9(6) *Finance and Credit Law* 3.

Davidson, R. (2007) 'The Companies Act 2006: directors' duties and promoting the company's success', 11 *Journal of International Banking and Finance Law* 631.

Drew, C. (1995) 'Financial services: The director's duties – an examination of directors' fiduciary duties following the issue of the Cadbury Code and the DTI's forthcoming review', 92(16) *Law Society Gazette*.

Killian, C. (2008) 'Some notes on the application of the doctrine of proper purpose', 29(2) *Company Lawyer* 61.

Riley, C. (1989) 'Directors' duties and the interests of creditors', 10(5) *Company Lawyer* 87.

Sealy, L. (2001) 'Directors' duties revisited', 22(3) *Company Lawyer* 79.

Spedding, L. (2004) 'Corporate governance issues', 3(5) *Advising Business* 11.

www.pearsoned.co.uk/lawexpress

 Go online to access more revision support including quizzes to test your knowledge, sample questions with answer guidelines, podcasts you can download, and more!

Corporate finance and charges

7

Revision checklist

Essential points you should know:

- [ ] The essential characteristics of shares and borrowing as sources of corporate finance
- [ ] The role of charges in securing debts of the company
- [ ] The distinction between fixed and floating charges and the characteristics of each
- [ ] The rules governing registration and priority of charges

■ Topic map

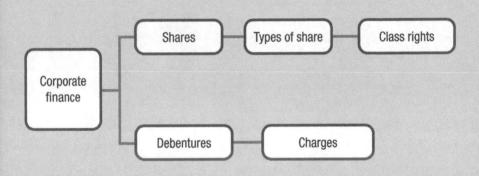

■ Introduction

Every business needs money and that money has to come from somewhere.

Any company, whether new or established, needs to raise finance at various stages in its lifetime. This might be when the company is first incorporated or later when it seeks to exploit new business ventures. One way of financing such opportunities is simply by retained profit but, if that is insufficient, then other avenues must be pursued and the most common mechanisms are shares and debentures.

ASSESSMENT ADVICE

There are two key aspects of this subject which are most frequently examined.

Essay questions

Essay questions usually ask you to compare shares and debentures as sources of corporate finance and this may also include consideration of charges as mechanisms for securing debts against the assets of the company.

Problem questions

Problem questions usually present a scenario involving both fixed and floating charges and ask you to consider the enforceability of the charges and the probable priority of repayment.

■ Sample question

Could you answer this question? Below is a typical problem question that could arise on this topic. Guidelines on answering the question are included at the end of this chapter, whilst a sample essay question and guidance on tackling it can be found on the companion website.

PROBLEM QUESTION

Michael and Ernie are the directors and majority shareholders of 'Chinaworks Ltd', which manufactures porcelain ornaments for export. In June 2007 they are advised by the company's accountant that the business is in serious difficulties due to the strength of the pound, which had made the company's products more expensive abroad. In the view of the accountant, the business will be insolvent within months. ▶

In September 2007 Chinaworks Ltd finds itself with 'temporary cashflow problems' and so Michael approaches the bank in order to increase the company's overdraft facility. An increased overdraft of £75,000 is duly agreed; however, as a condition of granting the overdraft, the bank insists on a 'first fixed charge' over the company's fixed assets together with a floating charge over the company's entire undertaking. In addition, the floating charge contains a restriction preventing the company from granting any other charge over its assets which ranks in priority or equal to the bank's charge, together with a clause which stipulates that the bank's floating charge will crystallise immediately in the event of the company attempting to grant a competing charge in favour of anyone else.

The company's fortunes briefly improve but, by the end of 2007, the company is again in crisis. In an attempt to keep it afloat Michael obtains a further loan of £20,000 from Loanshark Ltd which, before agreeing the loan, insists on a floating charge on the company's entire undertaking.

In February 2008 Michael and Ernie decide that the accountant was right after all and decide to wind up 'Chinaworks Ltd', leaving a large number of creditors unpaid. The value of the company's assets has yet to be fully assessed but they are clearly insufficient to meet the company's debts.

Discuss.

■ Shares

The topic of shares has already featured earlier but without any clear definition of what is meant by the term.

KEY CASE

Borland's Trustee v *Steel Bros & Co. Ltd* [1901] 1 Ch 279 (Ch)
Concerning: definition of a share

Facts

The facts of this case are lengthy and complicated and to summarise them here would add little to an understanding of the legal principle outlined below. Remember that examiners are usually looking for an understanding of the *ratio* and legal principle and that reciting the facts in an exam will not improve your grade.

Legal principle

Held: Farwell J: '[a share] is to be regarded as the interest of the shareholder in the company, measured, for the purposes of liability and dividend, by a sum of money.'

We know that most limited companies are limited by shares and that the amount paid (or owing) for shares represents the full extent of the personal liability of members for the debts of the company. They also usually confer the following rights on the shareholder:

- the right to a dividend of profit,
- the right to vote on important matters affecting the company,
- the right to repayment of capital on winding up of the company (once the company's debts have been paid).

 Make your answer stand out

Note that the ability of public companies to offer shares for sale to the public by means of prospectus is the most important distinction between private and public companies as it gives the latter access to enormous sums of money. This brings with it increased concerns over regulation, fraud and accountability which find expression in the debate over 'corporate governance'. For a discussion of the issues raised, see Maurer (2007).

Types of share

There are a number of types of share, the most important and common being *ordinary* and *preference* shares.

Ordinary shares

These are the standard or 'default' share in the company and usually confer one vote per share on the holder. They are entitled to a dividend from profit once any preference shareholders have received their dividend.

Preference shares

As the title suggests, the holders of preference shares receive some form of 'preference' or additional benefit over the holders of ordinary shares. This might take the form of an enhanced dividend compared to that which is paid to the ordinary shareholders, or priority to repayment of capital on winding up of the company.

 EXAM TIP

If you are discussing the different types of share it is worth spending a little time to mention that, although issuing preference shares may be a useful tool to entice reluctant investors, it also creates complications in that having both ordinary and preference shares increases both the administrative burden within the company and the possibility of antagonism between the different classes of shareholder.

Class rights

As indicated, shares have rights attached to them and this raises the question of whether the company can alter those rights against the wishes of the shareholders. Because altering the rights associated with the shares could reduce their value, this process of 'variation of **class rights**' is regulated by companies legislation.

KEY DEFINITION: Class rights

Those rights which are enjoyed by members of the company by virtue of their ownership of a particular class of shares.

KEY STATUTE

Companies Act 2006, section 630

Variation of class rights: companies having a share capital

. . .

(2) Rights attached to a class of a company's shares may only be varied –

   (a) in accordance with provision in the company's articles for the variation of those rights, or

   (b) where the company's articles contain no such provision, if the holders of shares of that class consent to the variation in accordance with this section.

. . .

(4) The consent required for the purposes of this section on the part of the holders of a class of a company's shares is –

   (a) consent in writing from the holders of at least three-quarters in nominal value of the issued shares of that class (excluding any shares held as treasury shares), or

   (b) a special resolution passed at a separate general meeting of the holders of that class sanctioning the variation.

The key element of the provisions is that any variation to class rights must either follow a procedure specified in the articles of association or be with the approval of the holders of the affected shares.

Identifying a variation of class rights

KEY CASE

White v *Bristol Aeroplane Co. Ltd* [1953] Ch 65 (CA)
Concerning: defining class rights

Facts

The company planned to issue bonus shares to the ordinary shareholders. This was challenged by the holders of existing preference shares who claimed that the votes attached to the new shares would dilute their voting influence which they argued was a 'class right'.

Legal principle

Held: the proposed issue of new shares did not affect the rights of the existing preference shareholders. It may impact on the enjoyment of the rights, by reducing their overall influence within the company, but not the rights themselves. Romer LJ: 'It cannot be said that the rights of ordinary shareholders would be affected by the issue of further ordinary capital; their rights would remain just as they were before, and the only result would be that the class of persons entitled to exercise those rights would be enlarged.'

KEY CASE

Greenhalgh v *Arderne Cinemas Ltd and Mallard* [1946] 1 All ER 512 (Ch)
Concerning: defining class rights

Facts

G lent a sum of money to the company in exchange for a number of 10p shares which each had one vote attached to them (as did the company's other 50p shares). The company later divided each of its 50p shares into five shares of 10p, with each share taking one vote each. This multiplied their voting power by five and so reduced G's voting influence within the company. G objected that this was a variation of his class rights.

Legal principle

Held: the class rights had not changed. Each share had enjoyed one vote before the change and continued to enjoy one vote afterwards. In this way, it was the enjoyment of the right, and not the right itself, which had been altered. Lord Greene MR: 'As a matter of law, I am quite unable to hold that, as a result of the transaction, the rights are varied; they remain what they always were – a right to have one vote per share.'

KEY CASE

Cumbrian Newspapers Group Ltd v *Cumberland & Westmoreland Herald Newspapers & Printing Co. Ltd* [1987] Ch 1 (Ch)

Concerning: variation of class rights

Facts

The claimant and defendant, which were both newspaper publishers, negotiated a deal where the defendant would buy one of the claimant's newspapers in exchange for 10 per cent of the defendant's share capital. The defendant issued the shares to the claimant and, as part of the deal, granted special rights to the shares by means of the articles of association. After several years, the directors tabled a resolution to cancel these special rights. The claimant objected, arguing that they were 'class rights'.

Legal principle

Held: the special rights granted by the articles were rights conferred on the claimant as a shareholder. Therefore, they were 'rights attached to a class of shares' and so could not be altered without the consent of the holders of those shares. Scott J: 'the shares in the defendant for the time being held by the plaintiff constitute a class of shares for the purpose of variation or abrogation of those rights.'

Objections to the variation

KEY STATUTE

Companies Act 2006, section 633

Right to object to variation: companies having a share capital

. . .

(2) The holders of not less in the aggregate than 15% of the issued shares of the class in question (being persons who did not consent to or vote in favour of the resolution for the variation) may apply to the court to have the variation cancelled.

. . .

(5) The court . . . may, if satisfied having regard to all the circumstances of the case that the variation would unfairly prejudice the shareholders of the class represented by the applicant, disallow the variation.

▉ Debentures

The other key source of corporate finance apart from shares is borrowing and this is often termed a 'debenture'. Under CA 2006, section 738, such debentures may be *unsecured* or *secured*. Unsecured borrowing usually takes the form of a simple overdraft facility from the bank but, for most companies, this is likely to be a relatively modest sum. For larger borrowing, it is necessary for the company to offer some security for the debt in the form of a *secured debenture* (i.e. secured against some asset of the company which can be seized if the debt is not repaid).

Debenture stock

An alternative to a secured debenture is 'debenture stock' which represents a series of loans from different lenders but on identical terms, usually by means of a trust deed administered by trustees, with the trustees acting as the link between the company and the lenders. The resulting 'debenture stock' can be traded in much the same way as shares.

Shares	Debentures
Shareholders are members of the company	Debenture holders are creditors of the company
The company cannot issue shares at a discount on the nominal value (CA 2006, s. 580)	The company is free to sell debentures at a discount
Shares usually entitle the holder to a dividend of profit	A debenture holder is only entitled to the agreed interest on the loan
There are restrictions on a public company purchasing its own shares (CA 2006, s. 678)	A company can purchase its own debentures free from restriction

✎ EXAM TIP

In discussing the differences between shareholders and debenture holders, it is useful to point out that the relationship between the company and the two groups is subtly different. Shareholders have an interest in the prosperity of the company because, if the company becomes more successful, their dividend is likely to increase. By contrast, no matter how successful the company is, all the debenture holders will get is the agreed interest on the loan.

Debentures and charges

Although debenture stock is a significant source of corporate finance, from the point of view of examination questions single debentures are a more common topic, particularly when coupled with a discussion of **charges**.

Charges

When a company fails and goes into liquidation, it is likely that there will not be sufficient assets to satisfy the claims of the company's creditors and that some will receive nothing. One way of avoiding this is for the creditor to seek a charge as a condition of making the loan. A charge is simply a mechanism for securing a debt against an asset so that, if the loan is not repaid, the lender can take the asset instead to satisfy the debt. This leads to the use of the term 'secured loan'. The securing of debts against assets in this way reduces the risk for the bank or other financial institution and so encourages them to lend money which they would not otherwise be willing to lend, due to the risk of default.

There are two types of charge – fixed and floating – and the effect of each is to increase the likelihood that the creditor will receive their money.

📖 **REVISION NOTE**

The use of charges to secure repayment of a creditor's claim should be considered alongside the provisions on insolvency discussed in Chapter 9.

Fixed charges

There are two types of charge and the most powerful is the **fixed charge**, which attaches to a physical asset of the company such as a building, land or vehicles. The key characteristic of a fixed charge is that the company holding the asset is unable to sell the asset without the consent of the lender. The most recognisable example of a fixed charge is the domestic mortgage, where a person borrows money from a bank or building society to buy a house but, in return, grants the lender a fixed charge over the property. If the repayments are not made, then the lender can repossess the property and sell it to satisfy the debt.

Floating charges

The restriction on the company being able to trade in the asset without the consent of the lender makes the fixed charge suitable for assets such as buildings (which the company is unlikely to sell very often) but less appropriate for assets such as raw materials or finished stock, which the company needs to buy and sell constantly. It is clearly impractical for the company to seek the approval of the lender each time it wishes to take some raw materials from the warehouse and so the **floating charge** is more suitable for such assets.

As the name suggests, the floating charge 'floats' over the class of assets but, crucially, the company does not need the consent of the lender to buy or sell the assets in question.

KEY CASE

Re Houldsworth v *Yorkshire Woolcombers Association Ltd* [1903]
2 Ch 284 (CA)

Concerning: characteristics of a floating charge

Facts

The facts of this case are lengthy and complicated and to summarise them here would add little to an understanding of the legal principle outlined below. Remember that examiners are usually looking for an understanding of the *ratio* and legal principle and that reciting the facts in an exam will not improve your grade.

Legal principle

Head: a floating charge has three essential characteristics: first, it is a charge on a class of assets of a company, present and future. Secondly, it is a class of assets which, in the ordinary course of the business of the company, would be changing from time to time. Thirdly, until some future step is taken by or on behalf of those interested in the charge, the company may deal with the assets in the usual way.

It is important to note, however, that the fact that the parties describe a charge as either 'fixed' or 'floating' is not conclusive, as demonstrated in the following case.

KEY CASE

Re Spectrum Plus Ltd [2005] UKHL 41

Concerning: charges

Facts

The company obtained an overdraft facility from the bank, secured by a debenture. Provided the overdraft limit was not exceeded, the company was free to draw on the account for its business purposes. When the company went into voluntary liquidation the bank applied for a declaration that the debenture had created a fixed charge over the company's book debts.

Legal principle

Held: although the debenture was expressed to grant the bank a fixed charge, in law it granted only a floating charge. The critical point was that the company was free to draw on the account pending notice by the bank terminating the overdraft facility. Its right to do so was inconsistent with the charge being a fixed charge and the label placed on the charge by the debenture did not affect this fact. Lord Nicholls: 'One must look, not at the declared intention of the parties alone, but to the effect of the instruments whereby they purported to carry out that intention.'

'Crystallisation'

The floating charge hangs over the class of assets, allowing the company to buy and sell them without consulting the lender. So when does the charge attach to the assets? The answer to this is when the floating charge 'crystallises' and falls on the particular assets which are present at that time. It has been held that **crystallisation** of a charge will occur in the following circumstances:

- on the company ceasing to trade,

- on liquidation of the company,

- on the appointment of a receiver to deal with the company's assets,

- on the occurrence of some event specified in the document creating the charge (e.g. default on the loan).

Registration

KEY STATUTE

Companies Act 2006, sections 860(1) and 874(1)

s. 860 Charges created by a company

(1) A company that creates a charge to which this section applies must deliver the prescribed particulars of the charge, together with the instrument (if any) by which the charge is created or evidenced, to the registrar for registration before the end of the period allowed for registration. [21 days]

s. 874 Consequence of failure to register charges created by a company

(1) If a company creates a charge to which section 860 applies, the charge is void (so far as any security on the company's property or undertaking is conferred by it) against –

(a) a liquidator of the company,

(b) an administrator of the company, and

(c) a creditor of the company,

unless that section is complied with.

EXAM TIP

Always remember to consider the issue of registration when answering any question on charges. Failure to register the charge renders it worthless and so can radically affect the outcome of a problem question.

Priority of charges

A common feature of examination questions on charges is whether the same assets may be subject to more than one charge. This raises the question of which charge will take priority. This is determined as follows:

■ two fixed charges – rank in order of creation;
■ two floating charges – rank in order of creation;
■ fixed charge followed by a floating charge – fixed charge takes priority;
■ floating charge followed by a fixed charge – fixed charge takes priority.

Negative pledge clauses

As stated in the final example above, a floating charge is defeated by a later fixed charge. This is because the fixed charge attaches to the asset on creation, whereas the floating charge only attaches on crystallisation. This means that a lender who secures a floating charge over a company's assets is vulnerable to the company granting another lender a fixed charge over the same assets at a later date.

To prevent this, it is common for the document granting a floating charge to include a clause stating that the company will not grant another charge over the same assets or, alternatively, that any attempt to grant such a charge will be taken as a 'crystallising event' for the purposes of the first floating charge. Such provisions are known as **negative pledge clauses**.

Avoiding charges

It is possible for liquidators to ignore charges under certain circumstances.

First, a floating charge may be ignored if it was granted immediately prior to the insolvency of the company.

KEY STATUTE

Insolvency Act 1986, ss. 245(2) and (3)

Avoidance of certain floating charges

(2) A floating charge on the company's undertaking or property created at a relevant time is invalid.

(3) The time at which a floating charge is created by a company is a relevant time for the purposes of this section if the charge is created –

    (a) in the case of a charge which is created in favour of a person who is connected with the company, at a time in the period of 2 years ending with the onset of insolvency,

    (b) in the case of a charge which is created in favour of any other person, at a time in the period of 12 months ending with the onset of insolvency.

Note that the period is longer for a 'connected person' (i.e. director or director's family, etc.) as they are assumed to have greater knowledge of the company's financial position and so may have attempted to secure a charge to increase their chances of repayment knowing that the company is heading towards insolvency.

It is also possible for any charge or other benefit to be avoided if it is deemed a 'preference' (i.e. an unfair advantage to an individual creditor designed to increase their chances of repayment over the other creditors).

KEY STATUTE

Insolvency Act 1986, ss. 239(2)–(4)

Preferences

(2) Where the company has . . . given a preference to any person, the office-holder may apply to the court for an order under this section.

(3) The court shall, on such an application, make such order as it thinks fit for restoring the position to what it would have been if the company had not given that preference.

(4) For the purposes of this section and section 241, a company gives a preference to a person if –

   (a) that person is one of the company's creditors or a surety or guarantor for any of the company's debts or other liabilities, and

   (b) the company does anything or suffers anything to be done which (in either case) has the effect of putting that person into a position which, in the event of the company going into insolvent liquidation, will be better than the position he would have been in if that thing had not been done.

✎ EXAM TIP

Insolvency Act (IA) 1986, ss. 239 and 245 are rarely mentioned in student answers on charges. Include reference to these provisions to show that you are aware of them, even if just to say, 'there is no indication that they apply in this case'.

■ Putting it all together

Answer guidelines

See the problem question at the start of the chapter.

Approaching the question

This is a fairly standard problem question which requires you to consider the validity of the various charges and determine which, if any, will take priority. Although the question is fairly lengthy it is, in fact, very straightforward.

Important points to include

As with any question, you should begin with a clear explanation of the relevant legal concepts, in this case charges. You should set out the purpose of charges (as a mechanism for securing a debt) and spend a little time outlining the position on insolvent liquidation, where the debts of the company outweigh the available assets. In such cases, the existence of a charge securing the debt may make the difference between the creditor receiving their money and receiving nothing. From here, you should outline the key characteristics of both fixed and floating charges.

Next you should consider the charges in the scenario. The crucial point is that there is no mention of any of the charges being registered and this is vital if the charge is to be effective. Therefore, you should consider the outcome in either eventuality, i.e. if the charges were registered and if they were not. If the charges were registered then the fixed charge will take priority and the negative pledge clause means that the first floating charge will take priority over the second. If the charges were not registered then none of the charges will be effective and the debts will be treated as unsecured.

 Make your answer stand out

- Emphasise the importance of both registration and the negative pledge clause.
- Recognise the possible application of IA 1986, section 214 (wrongful trading) in relation to continuing the business after being advised that it was insolvent.
- Mention the possible application of IA 1986, ss. 239 and 245, if only to discount them.

READ TO IMPRESS

Lawrence, J. (2008) 'Preferential creditors and floating charges', 23(1) *Journal of International Banking and Financial Law* 38.

Maurer, V. (2007) 'Corporate governance as a failsafe mechanism against corporate crime', 28(4) *Company Lawyer* 99.

Nolan, R.C. (2006) 'The continuing evolution of shareholder governance', 65(1) *Cambridge Law Journal* 92.

Sheehan, D. and Arvind, T.T. (2006) 'Prospective overruling and the fixed–floating charge debate', 122 *Law Quarterly Review* 20.

Worthington, S. (2001) 'Shares and shareholders: property, power and entitlement: Part 1', 22(9) *Company Lawyer* 258.

Worthington, S. (2008) 'Floating charges: the current state of play', 9 *Journal of International Banking and Financial Law* 467.

www.pearsoned.co.uk/lawexpress

Go online to access more revision support including quizzes to test your knowledge, sample questions with answer guidelines, podcasts you can download, and more!

Minority shareholder protection

8

Revision checklist

Essential points you should know:

☐ The relative position of minority shareholders within the company and the possible abuses committed by majority shareholders

☐ The theoretical basis for the rule in *Foss* v *Harbottle* (1843) 67 ER 189 (VC Ct) and the exceptions to the general rule

☐ The available remedies for minority shareholders under CA 2006, section 994 and the scope for derivative actions

☐ The possibility of 'just and equitable winding up' under IA 1986, section 122

■ Topic map

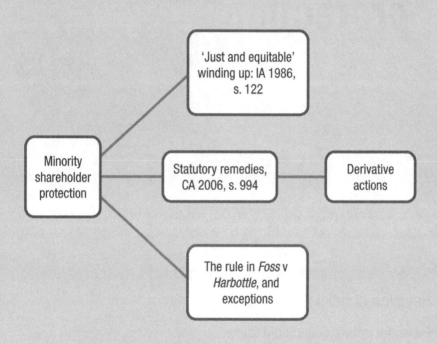

■ Introduction

When everything is decided by vote it can be difficult being in the minority.

We have already seen that many important decisions affecting the company are decided by a vote or 'resolution' passed by the members and, in this way, a company operates on an essentially democratic basis. Each share usually carries a vote and so those with the most shares (the 'majority shareholders') exercise the most votes. This does not cause problems when the majority shareholders cast their votes for the benefit of the company as a whole but, as we shall see, this is not always the case. Consequently, there is a need for company law to protect the interests of the minority shareholders.

ASSESSMENT ADVICE

Minority shareholder protection is another popular examination topic and lends itself to both essay and problem questions.

Essay questions

Essay questions might focus on the exceptions to the rule in *Foss* v *Harbottle* or petitions under what is now CA 2006, section 994 (formerly CA 1985, s. 459). Also, since CA 2006, questions may well ask you to consider the use of derivative actions under the new Act.

Problem questions

Problem questions may present a scenario where there is the possibility of wrongdoing by the majority shareholders. Here the question will require you to consider the various alternatives open to the minority shareholders, such as section 994 petitions and derivative actions and also, possibly, 'just and equitable winding up' under IA 1986, section 122.

■ Sample question

Could you answer this question? Below is a typical essay question that could arise on this topic. Guidelines on answering the question are included at the end of this chapter, whilst a sample problem question and guidance on tackling it can be found on the companion website.

Critically evaluate protections available to minority shareholders and their effectiveness in protecting the smaller shareholder from the unfair dominance of the majority.

■ The status of minority shareholders

Although the majority of shares in public companies (and particularly listed companies) are owned by the large 'institutional investors' (such as pension companies), there are also many individual shareholders, each of whom owns a small number of shares. Similarly, within private limited companies, there may be some members who own relatively few shares compared to others. In both cases, the fact that each share carries a single vote will usually mean that the smaller 'minority' shareholder cannot hope to defeat the majority shareholders in any vote affecting the company. It is important to recognise that this is not, in itself, undesirable or in any way sinister. It is simply a reflection of the democratic principle that underpins numerous aspects of everyday life which are decided by a vote. The side with the most votes wins and the losers accept that they were outvoted.

Within companies, however, problems may arise and these can be divided into two categories:

■ where the majority shareholders conspire to outvote the minority shareholders to achieve their own objectives;

■ when the majority shareholders are also the directors of the company and so are able to ratify any decision which they might take.

This second scenario in particular can cause serious problems for minority shareholders, as evidenced by the following decision.

KEY CASE

Foss v *Harbottle* (1843) 67 ER 189 (VC Ct)

Concerning: the 'proper plaintiff' rule

Facts

Two shareholders alleged wrongdoing on the part of the directors and began a court action on behalf of themselves and the other shareholders.

Legal principle

Held: individual members could not bring an action in this way as they had suffered no loss and so had no *locus standi*. The separate legal personality of the company meant that only the company could have suffered the loss and so only the company could bring an action. Held: 'In law the corporation and the aggregate members of the corporation are not the same thing for purposes like this.'

■ The rule in *Foss* v *Harbottle*

The result of this decision has become known as the 'rule in *Foss* v *Harbottle*', namely that the company itself (rather than an individual shareholder) is the 'proper plaintiff' in any action where there is an alleged wrong against the company. This is perfectly in keeping with the doctrine of corporate personality but is harsh for minority shareholders because very often it is the directors who have committed the alleged wrongdoing. As they are hardly likely to approve the company taking legal action against themselves this can leave the shareholders without an apparent remedy.

Exceptions to the rule

The following exceptions to the general rule have emerged under the common law.

Ultra vires act

Remember (from Chapter 5) that a member may still challenge an action which would be *ultra vires*, providing that the agreement has not been concluded.

Where the personal rights of a shareholder are involved

A shareholder can act against the company to enforce personal rights under the company's constitution.

> **□ REVISION NOTE**
>
> This raises the question of the 's. 33 contract' which regards the articles of association as the terms of a contract between the company and its members: see Chapter 5 (page 66).

> **KEY CASE**
>
> *Pender* v *Lushington* (1877) 6 ChD 70 (Ch)
> *Concerning: personal rights of members*
>
> **Facts**
>
> The constitution of the company provided that each member was entitled to a vote for every 10 shares they owned but only to a maximum of 100 votes. In order to avoid this rule, a member transferred some of his shares to another person who would use the votes on his behalf. When this was attempted at a meeting, the chairman of the meeting refused to accept the votes. ▶

Legal principle

Held: if the holder of the shares was listed on the register of the company's members (which he was) then this was all that was required. The votes of a shareholder who was properly registered could not be rejected just because the shares had been transferred to them by another shareholder for the purpose of increasing their own voting power. Jessel MR: 'the company has no right whatever to enter into the question of the beneficial ownership of the shares. Any such suggestion is quite inadmissible.'

Where a special majority is needed

If the company's constitution provides that a special majority is required to approve a particular action and the company ignores this requirement then an individual member may bring proceedings to challenge the vote.

KEY CASE

Edwards v *Halliwell* [1950] 2 All ER 1064 (CA)

Concerning: matters requiring a special resolution

Facts

The rules of the defendant trade union provided that the contributions of members could not be altered without a two-thirds majority vote of the members. Despite this, the union passed a resolution, without a vote, increasing the contributions of its members, two of whom challenged the legality of the action.

Legal principle

Held: as the matter was not a mere irregularity of the union's internal management, but was a matter of substance, the applicants could challenge the actions of the union. Asquith LJ: 'the individual members who are suing sue, not in the right of the union, but in their own right to protect from invasion their own individual rights as members.'

❗ Don't be tempted to . . .

Do not be confused by the fact that this case concerns a trade union rather than a limited company. The courts are prepared to recognise the similarities between the organisational structure and regulation of such bodies and extend general principles of shareholder democracy to the members of other such bodies (including unions).

Fraud by those controlling the company

The final recognised exception to the general rule concerned the situation where it is alleged that those in control of the company (i.e. the directors) have perpetrated a fraud. Under such circumstances, a member may bring a claim on behalf of the company known as a '**derivative claim**' (discussed below).

KEY CASE

Cook v *Deeks* [1916] 1 AC 554 (PC)

Concerning: fraud by directors

Facts

Three directors of the company obtained a contract in their own names to the exclusion of the company. This amounted to a breach of trust by the directors but, as holders of three-quarters of the issued shares, they later passed a resolution declaring that the company had no interest in the contract (thereby removing the conflict of interest).

Legal principle

Held: as the contract belonged to the company, the directors could not misuse their voting power to remove the company's interest. Lord Buckmaster LC: 'it appears quite certain that directors holding a majority of votes would not be permitted to make a present to themselves. This would be to allow a majority to oppress the minority.'

📖 **REVISION NOTE**

Note that this is a 'conflict of interest' situation as described in Chapter 6. Have another look at this area when considering this exception to the rule in *Foss* v *Harbottle*.

◼ Statutory remedies

Under the Companies Act 2006 there are now a series of statutory remedies available to minority shareholders. The most important of these are:

Claim	Relevant statutory provisions
Action for 'unfairly prejudicial conduct'	CA 2006, section 994
Derivative claim	CA 2006, section 260
'Just and equitable winding up'	IA 1986, section 122

Action for 'unfairly prejudicial conduct'

KEY STATUTE

Companies Act 2006, section 994(1)

Petition by company member

(1) A member of a company may apply to the court by petition for an order under this Part on the ground –

    (a) that the company's affairs are being or have been conducted in a manner that is unfairly prejudicial to the interests of members generally or of some part of its members (including at least himself), or

    (b) that an actual or proposed act or omission of the company (including an act or omission on its behalf) is or would be so prejudicial.

EXAM TIP

Note the requirement that the conduct is not only prejudicial to the rights of shareholders but also that it is *unfairly* prejudicial. This is important as anyone who loses a vote could claim that their interests have been prejudiced, but there is clearly nothing wrong with losing a vote. The issue is whether the shareholder has been treated unfairly, and the examiner will give you credit for making this distinction.

What is 'unfairly prejudicial'?

KEY CASE

Elder v *Elder & Watson Ltd* 1952 SC 49 (Ct of Sess)

Concerning: defining 'unfairly prejudicial'

Facts

The facts of this case are lengthy and complicated and to summarise them here would add little to an understanding of the legal principle outlined below. Remember that examiners are usually looking for an understanding of the *ratio* and legal principle and that reciting the facts in an exam will not improve your grade.

Legal principle

Held: Cooper LJ: 'the conduct complained of should at the lowest involve a visible departure from the standards of fair dealing, and a violation of the conditions of fair play on which every shareholder who entrusts his money to a company is entitled to rely.'

KEY CASE

Re London School of Electronics Ltd [1985] 3 WLR 474 (Ch)

Concerning: unfairly prejudicial conduct

Facts

The claimant was a 25 per cent shareholder in company A, which provided training courses. The remaining shares were held by company B, another training company. The majority shareholders and directors of company B were also directors of company A and caused students to be transferred from company A to company B in order to increase their own personal profit. The claimant, therefore, lost his share of the profit from the students taken by the other company.

Legal principle

Held: this conduct was unfairly prejudicial to the interests of the claimant as a minority shareholder. The majority shareholders had acted in their own interests. Nourse J: 'that was clearly conduct on the part of C.T.C. which was both unfair and prejudicial to the interests of the petitioner as a member of the company.'

KEY CASE

Re Sam Weller & Sons Ltd [1990] Ch 682 (Ch)

Concerning: defining 'unfair prejudice'

Facts

The company had paid the same low dividend for 37 years. The majority of the shares were owned by SW and his sons who were paid salaries by the company (and so were not dependent on the dividend). The claimant was a minority shareholder who received only the dividend and so argued that the business was being conducted for the personal benefit of SW and his sons to the detriment of the other minority shareholders.

Legal principle

Held: although the low dividend affected all of the company's shareholders, it clearly had less effect on those receiving a salary from the company. Therefore, the conduct could still be unfairly prejudicial against the minority shareholders. Gibson J: 'As their only income from the company is by way of dividend, their interests may be not only prejudiced by the policy of low dividend payments, but unfairly prejudiced.'

KEY CASE

O'Neill and another v *Phillips and another* **[1999] 1 WLR 1092 (HL)**

Concerning: unfairly prejudicial conduct

Facts

O worked for a construction company entirely owned by P. O became a minority shareholder and director of the company. It was suggested that he take a 50 per cent stake in the company but no actual agreement was made. Following a downturn in the construction industry, O was effectively excluded from the management of the company and consequently left. He subsequently made a claim under section 994.

Legal principle

Held: as P had made no actual promises regarding O's rights to shares and additional profit, there was no basis, consistent with the principles of equity, for a court to hold that P was behaving unfairly in withdrawing from the negotiation. Lord Hoffmann: 'the requirement that prejudice must be suffered as a member should not be too narrowly or technically construed. But the point does not arise because no promise was made.'

Derivative claim

A derivative claim is an action brought by an individual shareholder on behalf of the company (under the common law this was an exception to the rule in *Foss* v *Harbottle*). As has already been shown, this remedy existed for many years under the common law, but the scope for such actions has now increased dramatically with CA 2006 and the introduction of statutory provision for derivative actions.

KEY STATUTE

Companies Act 2006, ss. 260(3) and (4)

Derivative claims

(3) A derivative claim under this Chapter may be brought only in respect of a cause of action arising from an actual or proposed act or omission involving negligence, default, breach of duty or breach of trust by a director of the company. The cause of action may be against the director or another person (or both).

(4) It is immaterial whether the cause of action arose before or after the person seeking to bring or continue the derivative claim became a member of the company.

📖 REVISION NOTE

Note that the grounds for bringing a derivative action under CA 2006, section 260 include 'breach of duty or breach of trust by a director'. This is highly significant as it raises the prospect of actions for breach of the statutory directors' duties listed in Chapter 6. For this reason, you should examine the two areas together. Note also that an action can be brought by a member to challenge actions which occurred even before they became a shareholder in the company.

 Make your answer stand out

The use of derivative actions under CA 2006 is one of the most striking developments contained in the new statute and has attracted considerable comment. The examiner will give you credit for any background reading you can incorporate into your answer. For an overview, see Keay and Loughrey (2008), O'Neill (2007) and Ohrenstein (2007).

Factors to be considered

A number of factors must be considered by the court when deciding whether to allow a derivative action to proceed.

! Don't be tempted to . . .

Do not fall into the trap of assuming that anyone who wishes to bring a derivative action can do so. An action requires leave (permission) of the court and you should make this clear in any answer.

KEY STATUTE

Companies Act 2006, section 263(3)

(3) In considering whether to give permission (or leave) the court must take into account, in particular –

  (a) whether the member is acting in good faith in seeking to continue the claim;

  (b) the importance that a person acting in accordance with section 172 (duty to promote the success of the company) would attach to continuing it;

  (c) where the cause of action results from an act or omission that is yet to occur, whether the act or omission could be, and in the circumstances would be likely to be –

   (i) authorised by the company before it occurs, or

   (ii) ratified by the company after it occurs;   ▶

(d) where the cause of action arises from an act or omission that has already occurred, whether the act or omission could be, and in the circumstances would be likely to be, ratified by the company;

(e) whether the company has decided not to pursue the claim;

(f) whether the act or omission in respect of which the claim is brought gives rise to a cause of action that the member could pursue in his own right rather than on behalf of the company.

Just and equitable winding up

As an option of last resort, a member can petition for the company to be wound up.

KEY STATUTE

Insolvency Act 1986, section 122(1)(g)

Circumstances in which company may be wound up by the court

(1) A company may be wound up by the court if –

. . .

(g) the court is of the opinion that it is just and equitable that the company should be wound up.

Obviously this is a very serious course of action as it means that an otherwise successful company may be forced to cease trading. For this reason, the court will only make such an order in exceptional circumstances.

'Quasi-partnerships'

Many of the cases on just and equitable winding up concern 'quasi-partnership' companies. A 'quasi-partnership' company is a limited company which has a very small number of shareholders (usually two or three) and where all of the shareholders are also the directors of the company. Typically these are family companies. In this way, only those who have been involved in the management of the company stand to lose out as shareholders if the company is wound up.

When might a company be wound up under section 122(1)(g)?

KEY CASE

Ebrahimi v *Westbourne Galleries Ltd* [1973] AC 360 (HL)

Concerning: just and equitable winding up

Facts

E and N had operated as a partnership selling carpets and incorporated the business but their relationship deteriorated when N introduced his son into the business. Eventually N and his son removed E as a director, whereby E lost most of his income (as this had been in the form of his director's salary rather than from dividends).

Legal principle

Held: under the circumstances, it was just and equitable for the company to be wound up. Lord Wilberforce: 'All these matters lead only to the conclusion that the right course was to dissolve the association by winding up.'

KEY CASE

Re Yenidje Tobacco Co. Ltd [1916] 2 Ch 426 (CA)

Concerning: just and equitable winding up

Facts

The company had two shareholders who were also the directors. The relationship between the two became so difficult that they refused to speak to each other and had to communicate through the company secretary. As they both had equal voting power, it became impossible to pass any resolution affecting the company.

Legal principle

Held: under the circumstances, it was just and equitable for the company to be wound up. Warrington LJ: 'the court has in more cases than one expressed the view that a company may be wound-up if . . . the state of things is such that what may be called a deadlock has been arrived at in the management of the business of the company.'

KEY CASE

Re Blériot Manufacturing Air Craft Co. Ltd [1917] HBR 279 (Ch)

Concerning: just and equitable winding up

Facts

The company was incorporated to represent the well-known French aviator Louis Blériot in England. However, after the company was formed, Blériot refused to honour the contract.

Legal principle

Held: as the 'substratum' (the main purpose) of the company had failed, it was just and equitable that the company should be wound up.

! Don't be tempted to . . .

In examinations, many students suggest 'just and equitable' winding up as the first solution when faced with a minority shareholder problem. Remember that winding up an otherwise successful company is a drastic measure and, as such, should be considered as the *last*, rather than the first, resort.

■ Putting it all together

Answer guidelines

See the essay question at the start of the chapter.

Approaching the question

This is a standard essay question on the topic, which simply requires you to outline the various avenues available to minority shareholders and to offer some view on the effectiveness (or otherwise) of the provisions. The examiner will not be expecting great depth of analysis but you will need to show that you have actively considered the pros and cons of the various mechanisms for minority shareholder protection. In such answers, a clear structure is essential, so make sure that you plan the answer before you begin.

Important points to include

You should start by outlining the relationship between the majority and minority shareholders and the difficulties which can arise from an abuse of voting power by the majority shareholders. It is also useful to make a distinction at this point between the various types of company and the relative status of minority shareholders (e.g. minority shareholders within a public or listed company are likely to have little or no influence compared to those within small private companies – especially 'quasi-partnerships'). The next stage is to consider the rule in *Foss* v *Harbottle*, which is generally taken as the starting point for the discussion. After clearly explaining the rule, which obviously does not help minority shareholders, you should briefly consider the common law exceptions to the rule, such as *ultra vires*. The next key protection for minority shareholders is a petition under CA 2006, section 994 (formerly CA 1985, s. 459) and the concept of 'unfair prejudice'. You should emphasise the rather vague nature of this definition. From there, move on to discuss the scope for derivative actions under CA 2006, section 260, making clear that this represents a significant strengthening of shareholder rights. Finally, you should outline the circumstances where the court may consider making an order for the winding up of a company on 'just and equitable' grounds.

 Make your answer stand out

- Link derivative actions to the new directors' rights introduced by CA 2006 and make clear that this may well represent a new era of accountability for directors.

- Make clear the restricted circumstances in which an order will be granted under IA 1986, section 122(1)(g) – do not portray this as a routine solution for minority shareholders.

- Remember to offer some view on the effectiveness of the provisions. For example, the *ultra vires* exception to the rule in *Foss* v *Harbottle* is greatly undermined by the requirement that the application to the court must be made before the action complained of produces a valid contract.

READ TO IMPRESS

Bourne, N. (2002) 'Just and equitable winding up', 23(6) *Business Law Review* 138.

Keay, A. and Loughrey, J. (2008) 'Something old, something new, something borrowed: an analysis of the new derivative action under the Companies Act 2006', 124 *Law Quarterly Review* 469.

Mukwiri, J. (2004) 'Using section 459 as an instrument of oppression?', 25(9) *Company Lawyer* 282.

Ohrenstein, D. (2007) 'Derivative action', 157 *New Law Journal* 1372.

O'Neill, A. (2007) 'Reforming the derivative suit', 157 *New Law Journal* 356.

Payne, J. (2005) 'Sections 459–461 Companies Act 1985 in flux: the future of shareholder protection', 64(3) *Cambridge Law Journal* 647.

www.pearsoned.co.uk/lawexpress

 Go online to access more revision support including quizzes to test your knowledge, sample questions with answer guidelines, podcasts you can download, and more!

Liquidation

9

Revision checklist

Essential points you should know:

- [ ] The various methods by which a company may be brought to an end
- [ ] The distinction between insolvency and administration procedures
- [ ] The operation of voluntary arrangements, administration and liquidation procedures
- [ ] The priority of payment on the winding up of a company

■ Topic map

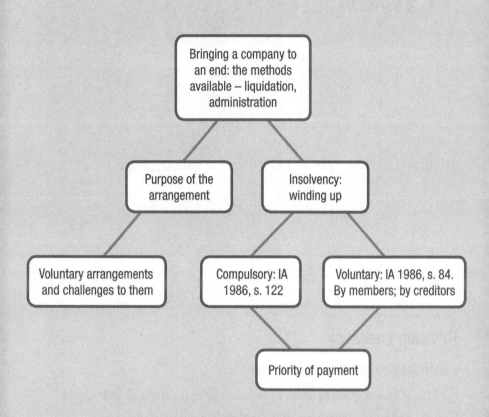

Bringing a company to an end: the methods available – liquidation, administration

Purpose of the arrangement

Insolvency: winding up

Voluntary arrangements and challenges to them

Compulsory: IA 1986, s. 122

Voluntary: IA 1986, s. 84. By members; by creditors

Priority of payment

A printable version of this topic map is available from **www.pearsoned.co.uk/lawexpress**

■ Introduction

If incorporation can be seen as the 'birth' of the company, then liquidation is its death.

We have used the concept of corporate personality to illustrate how a company is legally treated much as an individual would be. The process of incorporation provides the company with a legal status separate from its promoters as long as the company is in existence. This ends with the liquidation of the company, where the affairs of the business are settled and its assets distributed to those entitled to them.

ASSESSMENT ADVICE

As with many of the previous topics, liquidation lends itself readily to both essay and problem questions.

Essay questions

Essay questions may ask you to consider the various mechanisms for ending a company and the relative protection which each procedure provides for parties such as creditors and shareholders.

Problem questions

Problem questions may present the scenario of an insolvent company facing liquidation and ask you to advise on the most appropriate course of action.

■ Sample question

Could you answer this question? Below is a typical essay question that could arise on this topic. Guidelines on answering the question are included at the end of this chapter, whilst a sample problem question and guidance on tackling it can be found on the companion website.

ESSAY QUESTION

Outline the various ways in which an insolvent company may be brought to an end; and to what extent do the different mechanisms safeguard the interests of creditors?

■ Purpose of the process

When a company is in financial difficulty, there are a number of different processes which can be employed to bring the company to an end, but there are also procedures which can be used to achieve certain objectives without necessarily ending the company. Most of these involve passing ownership and control of the company from the shareholders and directors (respectively) to a qualified *insolvency practitioner*, who deals with the assets of the company on behalf of the company's creditors. However, the precise nature of this transfer depends on the mechanism used. This requires you to appreciate the difference between *liquidation* and *administration*.

Liquidation

The purpose of liquidation is to end the company as a separate legal personality and to bring it to a close. The company will cease to exist and the purpose of the liquidation is to settle the company's affairs, paying as many of its debts as possible (depending on the funds available) and distributing the remainder (if any) to the shareholders. The extent to which this is possible depends on whether it is a 'solvent liquidation' (where the assets outnumber the debts) or an 'insolvent liquidation' (where the debts outnumber the assets). Clearly the latter is the most common and, in such cases, not only will the shareholders receive nothing but also many of the company's creditors will get nothing as well.

Administration

The aim of administration is slightly different in that it seeks to facilitate the rescue of the company by placing it in the hands of the administrator whose role is, where possible, to save the company as a going concern. During this time the creditors are not able to commence winding up proceedings without leave of the court. If it proves impossible to save the company then the administrator seeks to maximise the return to creditors. The aim of the process is to achieve a better result than would be possible if the company were to be immediately placed into liquidation.

> ✎ **EXAM TIP**
>
> Many students fail to make this distinction absolutely clear and become confused as to what the two processes are designed to achieve. Ensure that you take a little time to explain this in your answer.

Clearly the appropriate course of action will depend on the individual circumstances of the company in question. We will begin by considering those procedures which at least attempt to leave the company as a going concern before examining those which inevitably result in the 'death' of the company.

◼ Voluntary arrangements

One of the simplest ways in which a company in financial difficulty may attempt to survive is by means of an arrangement with its creditors. This may entail the creditors receiving an agreed proportion of what they are owed or entering into a 'scheme of arrangement'.

KEY STATUTE

Insolvency Act 1986, ss. 1(1) and (3)

(1) The directors of a company (other than one which is in administration or being wound up) may make a proposal under this Part to the company and to its creditors for a composition in satisfaction of its debts or a scheme of arrangement of its affairs.

. . .

(3) Such a proposal may also be made –

(a) where the company is in administration, by the administrator, and

(b) where the company is being wound up, by the liquidator.

Procedure

Stage	Comment
Proposal put forward for voluntary arrangement with creditors, including the appointment of a 'nominee'	The nominee is the insolvency practitioner who will supervise the making of the arrangement between the company and its creditors
Nominee confirms to the court that the proposal should be considered by a meeting of the company's creditors	The court does not approve the actual proposal
The nominee arranges a meeting of the company's creditors to consider the proposal	The creditors may make alterations to the proposal but not radically change it
The proposal is approved by the company's shareholders	Once approved, the agreement is binding on the parties
The nominee supervises the conduct of the arrangement	

Challenging the arrangement

Under IA 1986, section 6 an arrangement may be challenged by a shareholder or creditor on the basis of 'unfair prejudice'.

KEY CASE

IRC v *Wimbledon Football Club Ltd and others* [2005] 1 BCLC 66 (CA)

Concerning: unfair prejudice

Facts

The facts of this case are lengthy and complicated and to summarise them here would add little to an understanding of the legal principle outlined below. Remember that examiners are usually looking for an understanding of the *ratio* and legal principle and that reciting the facts in an exam will not improve your grade.

Legal principle

Held: to constitute a good ground of challenge the unfair prejudice complained of must be caused by the terms of the arrangement itself. This might include the unequal or differential treatment of creditors of the same class. Such unequal treatment is not of itself unfair, but it does require an explanation. Lightman J: 'I can see no unfairness in the arrangement so far as it provides for payment in full of the priority creditors by the buyer.'

EXAM TIP

Although this is not 'minority shareholder protection' as such, the examiner will be impressed by an answer which draws a parallel between the two areas.

■ Administration

As stated above, unlike liquidation, the aim of administration is not to end the company.

KEY STATUTE

Insolvency Act 1986, Schedule B1, paragraph 3(1)

3(1) The administrator of a company must perform his functions with the objective of –

(a) rescuing the company as a going concern, or

(b) achieving a better result for the company's creditors as a whole than would be likely if the company were wound up (without first being in administration), or

(c) realising property in order to make a distribution to one or more secured or preferential creditors.

Make your answer stand out

The law relating to administration has been subject to considerable revision after the Enterprise Act 2002 and some reference to this will be sure to enhance the quality of your answer. For an overview of the key changes and the theoretical background, see Finch (2003) and Frisby (2007) (two-part article).

Procedure

Stage	Comment
An administrator is appointed	This can be done (out of court) by the company itself, by the directors or by the holder of a floating charge granted by the company over some of its assets. Alternatively, any of the above may ask the court to appoint (note that, before the court will appoint an administrator, it must be satisfied that the company is, or is likely to be, unable to pay its debts)
The administrator presents proposals to creditors, shareholders and the Registrar of Companies	This must be done within eight weeks of appointment
A creditors' meeting is held to consider the proposals	A simple majority (by value of debt) is required
If accepted, the administrator manages the company in order to achieve the agreed objectives	In doing so, the administrator takes over from the directors, who lose control of the company
The administration terminates automatically after 12 months	This period can be extended indefinitely by the court

 Don't be tempted to . . .

The current provisions on administration replace the previous system of appointing an 'administrative receiver'. However, this remains significant as the holder of a floating charge over the company's assets granted before September 2003 may still be entitled to use the old procedure to recover their money. The key difference is that the ▶

administrative receiver acts for the holder of the charge and their objective is to realise the money from the company's assets to repay the debenture covered by the charge. It was also possible for an administrative receiver to be appointed by the court and, in such circumstances, the receiver acts as an officer of the court rather than on behalf of any particular creditor. As the new procedures are in force, it is unlikely that an examiner would expect you to discuss the old process in any detail, but a passing reference will demonstrate your knowledge of the area.

Insolvency

A company is deemed insolvent if it is unable to pay its debts or if its liabilities are greater than its assets. Where the court is satisfied that either of these circumstances exists, an order may be made for the company to be wound up. Also, if the court is satisfied that either of these circumstances is likely to apply in the near future, an administrator may be appointed to manage the company's affairs as described above.

Winding up

There are a number of ways in which a company may be wound up. Some are compulsory and some are voluntary.

Compulsory winding up

Under IA 1986, section 122 the court may order a company to be wound up, *inter alia*, where:

- the members have passed a special resolution that the company should be wound up (s. 122(1)(a));
- the company is a public company and has not been issued with a certificate of minimum share capital and more than a year has passed since registration (s. 122(1)(b));
- the company does not commence business for a year after registration or suspends its business for a year (s. 122(1)(d));
- the company is unable to pay its debts (s. 122(1)(f));
- the court is of the opinion that it is 'just and equitable' that the company should be wound up (s. 122(1)(g)).

> 📖 **REVISION NOTE**
>
> Note that we earlier discussed section 122(1)(g) in Chapter 8 as part of the protection available to minority shareholders.

Re ABC Coupler & Engineering Co. Ltd [1961] 1 All ER 354 (Ch)

Concerning: consideration of applications

Facts

One creditor petitioned for the company to be wound up in order to recover their debt; however, the petition was opposed by a number of the company's other creditors.

Legal principle

Held: the application would be refused. The court was not obliged to grant an order and had a discretion to refuse. Pennycuick J: 'if it is thought right to take account of the wishes of the majority of the creditors, and if those wishes are reasonable, then the court can properly refuse at their request to make a winding-up order.'

Voluntary winding up

Under IA 1986, section 84 a company may be wound up voluntarily where:

- the period (if any) fixed for the duration of the company by the articles expires;
- the company resolves by special resolution that it be wound up voluntarily;
- the company resolves by extraordinary resolution to the effect that it cannot by reason of its liabilities continue its business, and that it is advisable to wind up.

There are two types of voluntary winding up – 'creditors' voluntary winding up' and 'members' voluntary winding up'.

Members' voluntary winding up

This requires the directors to make a 'declaration of solvency'.

Insolvency Act 1986, section 89(1)

Statutory declaration of solvency

(1) Where it is proposed to wind up a company voluntarily, the directors . . . may make a statutory declaration to the effect that they have made a full inquiry into the company's affairs and that, having done so, they have formed the opinion that the company will be able to pay its debts in full . . . within such period, not exceeding 12 months from the commencement of the winding up, as may be specified in the declaration.

After the statutory declaration, there is a general meeting of the company's members at which a resolution is passed to wind up the company and appoint a liquidator who immediately takes over the management of the company.

The role of the liquidator is to realise the assets of the company and distribute them between the various creditors *pari passu* (in proportion to the amount they are owed).

Creditors' voluntary winding up

Where there is no statutory declaration of solvency, the liquidation proceeds as a creditors' voluntary winding up.

! Don't be tempted to . . .

Be careful to make clear that a members' voluntary liquidation can occur only after the production of a statutory declaration of solvency. Don't neglect this point, because the statutory declaration is very important as it confirms to the company's creditors that the company will be able to pay its debts for the coming months.

Therefore, if no such declaration is forthcoming, the creditors must pursue the liquidation to protect themselves.

In terms of procedure, this also requires the shareholders to pass a resolution calling for the company to be wound up and appointing a liquidator. In turn, the liquidator must call a creditors' meeting to approve the proposal for the voluntary winding up. The creditors may also appoint a 'liquidation committee' to liaise with the liquidator over the management of the company's affairs. The role of the liquidator remains to realise the assets of the company and distribute these as appropriate.

Priority of payment

On liquidation of the company, the priority of payment is as follows:

- the liquidation costs (including the liquidator's fee),
- any preferential creditors (such as wages due to the company's employees and any outstanding pension contributions),
- any floating charges,
- any unsecured creditors,
- any remainder is distributed amongst the shareholders.

■ Putting it all together

Answer guidelines

See the essay question at the start of the chapter.

Approaching the question

This is a straightforward essay question, which requires you to demonstrate a sound knowledge of the various alternatives facing companies in difficulty. This is a complex area and the examiner will not be expecting exhaustive detail from you, but what you do need to show is both a firm grasp of the basic differences between administration, liquidation, voluntary arrangements, etc. and some element of analysis which places the various procedures within a context of safeguarding the interests of those involved. One danger is that this is a topic where it is possible to write a 'common sense' answer which contains little law and, consequently, earns few marks, so students would be well advised not to tackle this topic if they are not clear on the relevant provisions.

Important points to include

You should begin by outlining the nature of failing companies and the fact that, in many cases, the result is an 'insolvent liquidation' where the assets of the company are far outweighed by its liabilities. This means that not all of the company's creditors will receive their money back and so there must be some process of realising as many of the company's assets as possible. You should also make clear the distinction between processes designed to bring the company to an end immediately and those which aim to manage the company for a period of time in order to maximise the return to creditors. Next, you should consider processes such as voluntary arrangements and administration, which do not necessarily result in the end of the company, and consider whether these might ultimately benefit creditors. For example, whereas the creditors may receive something if the company is wound up immediately, they may receive more if the company is allowed to continue, providing that there are business opportunities which the company can exploit to bring in more revenue. Here it is worth mentioning the role of the administrator who assumes responsibility for the management of the company from the directors in order to supervise the implementation of any arrangement which has been agreed. You should also note the role of the creditors in approving any such arrangement. After all, it is their money at stake!

▶

The next step is to consider liquidation procedures and the grounds on which the company may be wound up. Here it is essential to make the distinction between compulsory winding up by the court and voluntary winding up, whether by members or creditors. Again, you might comment on the role of the liquidator as guardian of the creditors' interests, attempting to maximise their return by the sale of the company's assets.

Finally, offer some view on the effectiveness of the provisions. This does not need to be at a high level of analysis but needs to demonstrate that you can assess the relative advantages and disadvantages of the various mechanisms. For example, one simple point to make is that the administration and voluntary arrangement procedures not only allow the company to exploit any outstanding contracts in order to bring in more funds for creditors but also leave open the possibility that the company may actually survive once the procedure is completed.

 Make your answer stand out

- Point out the role of the 'statutory declaration of solvency' in a members' voluntary winding up as a safeguard for the interests of creditors.

- Emphasise the fact that the members of the company are usually unlikely to receive anything once the liquidation procedure is completed.

- Do not forget to include the priority of payment for creditors. The examiner will be pleased to see that you can assess, even in general terms, who is likely to be repaid and who is not.

READ TO IMPRESS

Elwes, S. (2005) 'Limitations on presenting a petition for the winding-up of a company', 21 *Tolley's Insolvency Law and Practice* 42.

Finch, V. (2003) 'Re-invigorating corporate rescue', *Journal of Business Law* 527.

Frisby, S. (2007) 'Not quite warp factor 2 yet? The Enterprise Act and corporate insolvency (pt. 1)', 6 *Journal of International Banking and Finance Law* 327.

Frisby, S. (2007) 'Not quite warp factor 2 yet? The Enterprise Act and corporate insolvency (pt. 2)', 7 *Journal of International Banking and Finance Law* 398.

Hill, A. (2006) 'Schemes of arrangement: binding unknown creditors in respect of unknown liabilities for unknown amounts', 8 *Journal of International Banking and Finance Law* 341.

McDermott, C. (2004) 'Overview of the effects of the new administration procedure', 6(5) *Finance and Credit Law* 1.

Sacks, C. (2007) 'Winding up a company', 893 *Tax Journal* 19.

www.pearsoned.co.uk/lawexpress

 Go online to access more revision support including quizzes to test your knowledge, sample questions with answer guidelines, podcasts you can download, and more!

And finally, before the exam . . .

Test yourself

☐ Look at the **revision checklists** at the start of each chapter. Are you happy that you can now tick them all? If not, go back to the particular chapter and work through the material again. If you are still struggling, seek help from your tutor.

☐ Attempt the **sample questions** in each chapter and check your answers against the guidelines provided.

☐ Go online to **www.pearsoned.co.uk/lawexpress** for more hands-on revision help and try out these resources:

  ☐ Try the **test your knowledge** quizzes and see if you can score full marks for each chapter.

  ☐ Attempt to answer the **sample questions** for each chapter within the time limit and check your answers against the guidelines provided.

  ☐ Listen to the **podcast** and then attempt the question it discusses.

  ☐ **You be the marker** and see if you can spot the strengths and weaknesses of the sample answers.

  ☐ Use the **flashcards** to test your recall of the legal principles of the key cases and statutes you've revised and the definitions of important terms.

☐ Look again at the key statutory provisions relating to each topic and, in particular, consider the relevant provisions of CA 2006. Do you know when and how these apply?

■ Linking it all up

Check where there are overlaps between subject areas. (You may want to review the 'revision note' boxes throughout this book.) Make a careful note of these as knowing how one topic may lead into another can increase your marks significantly. Here are some examples:

✔ Directors' duties and the minority shareholder protection measure of 'derivative actions'.

✔ Pre-incorporation contracts as an example of 'lifting the veil'.

✔ 'Just and equitable winding up' as a mechanism for minority shareholder protection and also as an insolvency measure.

✔ Floating charges as a means of securing a debt but also as a trigger for winding up the company.

■ Knowing your cases

Make sure you know how to use relevant case law in your answers. Use the table below to focus your revision of the key cases in each topic. To review the details of these cases, refer back to the particular chapter.

Key case	How to use	Related topics
Chapter 1 – Companies and other trading structures		
No relevant cases		
Chapter 2 – Incorporation		
Reckitt and Colman v *Borden*	To illustrate the requirements of an action for passing off	Company names/ passing off
Chapter 3 – Limited liability and corporate personality		
Salomon v *Salomon & Co.*	The leading decision on the company as a legal entity separate from its owners	Corporate personality
Macaura v *Northern Assurance Co.*	To illustrate the doctrine of corporate personality	Corporate personality
Lee v *Lee's Air Farming*	To illustrate the doctrine of corporate personality	Corporate personality

Key case	How to use	Related topics
Re Patrick Lyon Ltd	To define 'fraud' for the purposes of IA 1986, section 213	Corporate personality/ fraudulent trading
Re Produce Marketing Consortium Ltd	To set out the requirements for liability for wrongful trading under IA 1986, section 214	Corporate personality/ wrongful trading
Gilford Motor Co. v Horne	To show an example of a 'sham/ façade' company	Corporate personality/'sham/ façade' companies
Jones v Lipman	To show an example of a 'sham/ facade' company	Corporate personality/'sham/ facade' companies
The Albazero	To separate corporate personality for parent and subsidiary companies	Corporate personality/ groups of companies
Smith, Stone & Knight v Birmingham Corpn	To show an example of the 'single economic entity' argument	Corporate personality/ groups of companies
DHN v Tower Hamlets LBC	To show an example of the 'single economic entity' argument	Corporate personality/ groups of companies
Woolfson v Strathclyde Regional Council	To show the limitations of the 'single economic entity' argument	Corporate personality/ groups of companies
Adams v Cape Industries	To show the limitations of the 'single economic entity' argument	Corporate personality/ groups of companies
Tesco Supermarkets Ltd v Nattrass; Tesco Stores Ltd v Brent London Borough Council	Two cases which clarify the scope of the 'directing mind and will' of the company	Corporate personality/ liability

Chapter 4 – Pre-incorporation contracts

Kelner v Baxter	To demonstrate an example of the personal liability of the promoters	Corporate personality/ pre-incorporation contracts

▶

Key case	How to use	Related topics
Chapter 4 – Pre-incorporation contracts *Continued*		
Newborne v *Sensolid Ltd*	To demonstrate the importance of the manner of the signature	Corporate personality/ pre-incorporation contracts
Phonogram v *Lane*	To show the first application of section 51	Corporate personality/ pre-incorporation contracts
Braymist Ltd v *Wise Finance Co. Ltd*	Recognised that, as well as imposing liability, section 51 also conferred the right to sue	Corporate personality/ pre-incorporation contracts
Oshkosh B'Gosh Inc. v *Dan Marbel Inc. Ltd*	To illustrate that a change of company name did not create a 'new' company for the purposes of section 51	Corporate personality/ pre-incorporation contracts
Chapter 5 – The constitution of the company		
Ashbury Railway Carriage Co. v *Riche*	To show that a contract outside the terms of the company's objects clause was *ultra vires*	*Ultra vires*
Re German Date Coffee Co.	To show that a contract outside the terms of the company's objects clause was *ultra vires*	*Ultra vires*
Hickman v *Kent or Romney Marsh Sheepbreeders' Assoc.*	To demonstrate that the terms of the articles of association represented binding terms between the company and its members	Contractual nature of the company's constitution
Rayfield v *Hands*	To illustrate that the contractual principle of the articles also applied to an obligation to purchase shares	Contractual nature of the company's constitution
Beattie v *Beattie Ltd*	To demonstrate that the terms of the articles were only enforceable in relation to shareholders' rights	Contractual nature of the company's constitution
Allen v *Gold Reefs of West Africa Ltd*	Alterations to the articles must be in the interests of the company	Alteration of the articles

---

Key case	How to use	Related topics
Brown v *British Abrasive Wheel*	Alterations to the articles must be in the interests of the company	Alterations of the articles
Walker v *London Tramways*	The company cannot 'entrench' provisions within the articles of association	Alterations of the articles

Chapter 6 – Directors

Key case	How to use	Related topics
Gemma Ltd v *Davies*	To define a '*de facto*'/ '*shadow*' director	Directors
Re Paycheck Services 3 Ltd v *Holland*	To define a '*de facto*'/ '*shadow*' director	Directors
Hogg v *Cramphorn*	To consider conflict between the '*bona fide*' and 'proper purpose' duties	Directors' duties
Re Smith & Fawcett Ltd	To define the common law duty to act *bona fide*	Directors' duties
Regentcrest v *Cohen*	To define the common law duty to act *bona fide*	Directors' duties
Boulting v *Association of Cinematograph Television and Allied Technicians*	Clarifies the duty to exercise independent judgement	Directors' duties
Dorchester Finance v *Stebbing*	To define the common law duty of care and skill	Directors' duties
IDC Ltd v *Cooley*	To consider the duty to avoid conflicts of interest	Directors' duties/ corporate opportunity doctrine
CMS Dolphin Ltd v *Simonet*	To consider the duty to avoid conflicts of interest	Directors' duties/ corporate opportunity doctrine/maturing business opportunity

▶

Key case	How to use	Related topics
Chapter 6 – Directors *Continued*		
Island Export Finance Ltd v *Umunna*	To consider the duty to avoid conflicts of interest in the case of former employers	Directors' duties/ corporate opportunity doctrine
Boston Deep Sea Fishing v *Ansell*	To consider the equitable nature of the duty to avoid conflicts of interest	Directors' duties/ corporate opportunity doctrine
Chapter 7 – Corporate finance and charges		
Borland's Trustee v *Steel Bros & Co. Ltd*	To provide the legal definition of a 'share'	Share capital
White v *Bristol Aeroplane Co. Ltd*	To define 'class rights'	Share capital/class rights
Greenhalgh v *Arderne Cinemas Ltd*	To define 'class rights'	Share capital/class rights
Cumbrian Newspapers v *Cumbrian & Westmoreland Herald Newspapers*	To define 'class rights'	Share capital/class rights
Re Houldsworth v *Yorkshire Woolcombers Assoc.*	To define a floating charge	Debentures/charges
Re Spectrum Plus Ltd	Emphasises that the form of charge is determined by its effects, not the name given to it	Debentures/charges
Chapter 8 – Minority shareholder protection		
Foss v *Harbottle*	To clarify the 'proper plaintiff' principle	Minority shareholder protection/*locus standi*
Pender v *Lushington*	To consider the personal rights attached to the ownership of shares	Minority shareholder protection/personal rights

Key case	How to use	Related topics
Edwards v *Halliwell*	To consider the requirements of a special majority	Minority shareholder protection/personal rights/special majorities
Cook v *Deeks*	To consider remedies for fraud by those in control of the company	Minority shareholder protection/fraud
Elder v *Elder & Watson Ltd*	To give the definition of 'unfairly prejudicial'	Minority shareholder protection/unfairly prejudicial conduct
Re London School of Electronics Ltd	To give the definition of 'unfairly prejudicial'	Minority shareholder protection/unfairly prejudicial conduct
Re Sam Weller Ltd	To give the definition of 'unfairly prejudicial'	Minority shareholder protection/unfairly prejudicial conduct
O'Neill and another v *Phillips and another*	To give the definition of 'unfairly prejudicial' and the application of CA 2006 section 994	Minority shareholder protection/unfairly prejudicial conduct
Ebrahimi v *Westbourne Galleries*	To show the application of 'just and equitable' winding up	Minority shareholder protection/'just and equitable' winding up
Re Yenidje Tobacco Co. Ltd	To show the application of 'just and equitable' winding up	Minority shareholder protection/'just and equitable' winding up
Re Blériot Manufacturing Air Craft Co. Ltd	To show the application of 'just and equitable' winding up	Minority shareholder protection/'just and equitable' winding up

Chapter 9 – Liquidation

IRC v *Wimbledon Football Club*	To show unfair prejudice in the winding up process	Winding up
Re ABC Coupler	To set out the judicial discretion to refuse an application	Winding up

Sample question

Below is a problem question that incorporates overlapping areas of the law. See if you can answer this question drawing upon your knowledge of the whole subject area. Guidelines on answering this question are included at the end of this section.

PROBLEM QUESTION

Joan and Barbara have, for many years, operated a stall in the local market selling dressmaking materials. As their business was well established they decided to open a shop in the high street called 'Buttons & Bows' and persuaded a number of friends and family to invest money in the venture.

Conscious that they would need to make a profit as soon as the shop opened, Joan put a number of measures into place beforehand. She ordered all of the company's stationery, packaging materials and stock. She also leased a delivery van and had the 'Buttons & Bows' logo professionally painted on it. They had already opened a bank account in the name of 'The Buttons & Bows Partnership' and it was with cheques from this account that the goods were eventually paid for (the suppliers having granted Joan 90 days to pay). Joan and Barbara had always considered themselves 'partners' in business and so thought this would be a good name for their new enterprise.

Once the shop had opened, however, they were advised that they should form a limited company in order to put things on a 'proper' footing. Heeding this advice, they bought an 'off the shelf' company which became 'Buttons & Bows Ltd', and made each of the investors shareholders. Although Joan was happy to form the company, Barbara was extremely reluctant to become a director as she had been disqualified some years earlier after a disastrous business venture with her former husband. For this reason, Joan agreed to effectively run the business with Barbara remaining 'in the background'. However, they still considered themselves to be 'partners' in the business.

Almost from the outset the business began to fail as neither Joan nor Barbara had the business expertise to manage the more complex operation. After only three weeks Barbara decided that it had all been a mistake and fled to Malta, leaving Joan to struggle alone, at which point the other investors warned her that the situation was 'hopeless'. However, she was determined to make a success of the business and managed to negotiate further credit from her suppliers. Despite this, after another two months, the bank refused to extend the company's overdraft facility and she was forced to close the shop. At this point the company has virtually no assets and a mountain of debts.

Advise Joan and Barbara.

Answer guidelines

Approaching the question

This is a straightforward problem question, but one which raises a number of different areas which we have addressed in this text. The key to answering problem questions is always to take the scenario step by step and assess whether each development raises new legal issues which need to be addressed.

Important points to include

In this scenario, it is clear that the women begin their enterprise as a partnership but decide to incorporate as a private limited company. There are, however, issues surrounding the name 'partnership' and the refusal to adopt the Ltd suffix which may give customers a misleading impression of the status of the business (i.e. as a partnership with unlimited personal liability, rather than a private limited company with limited liability). Also, there is a clear pre-incorporation contract situation in relation to the stationery, packing materials, etc., which are ordered before the company is validly incorporated. This requires an application of CA 2006, section 51. There is also the problem that Barbara appears to be disqualified from acting as a director.

The inability of Joan and Barbara to manage the company effectively may suggest a breach of the directors' duties contained in CA 2006, section 174 and their refusal to take notice of warnings that the company may be heading for insolvency raises the possibility of wrongful trading under IA 1986, section 214.

There is also the question of whether the company should be placed into immediate liquidation or whether administration would be preferable. This will depend on the extent to which the company may be able to increase its assets by trading for an additional period and this information is not given. However, the examiner will give you credit for at least considering the various options.

 Make your answer stand out

- Emphasise that, as a disqualified director, Barbara should have taken no part in the promotion and management of the company.
- Spend some time considering whether there has been wrongful trading under IA 1986, section 214 and make clear that there is no evidence of fraudulent trading under IA 1986, section 213.
- Do explain the liquidation options available and consider whether administration may be a preferable option.

Glossary of terms

The glossary is divided into two parts: key definitions and other useful terms. The key definitions can be found within the chapter in which they occur, as well as in the glossary below. These definitions are the essential terms that you must know and understand in order to prepare for an exam. The additional list of terms provides further definitions of useful terms and phrases which will also help you answer examination and coursework questions effectively. These terms are highlighted in the text as they occur but the definition can only be found here.

■ Key definitions

Class rights	Those rights which are enjoyed by members of the company by virtue of their ownership of a particular class of shares.
Corporate personality	The separate legal status of a registered company which provides it with an identity which is separate from that of its members, shareholders and employees.
Novation	The replacement of one contract with another.
Objects clause	The clause within the company's constitution which states what the purpose of the company is to be.
Passing off	An action alleging that the defendant has 'passed off' their goods, services or business as that of the claimant, thereby taking advantage of the reputation or goodwill attached to the claimant's business.
Promoter	The person (or persons) who initially incorporate the company. They are the first shareholders and often also the directors. They have the ability to draft the company's memorandum and articles and so can shape the structure and direction of the company.
Registrar of Companies	Based at Companies House, the Registrar supervises the incorporation and dissolving of limited companies, collects and stores certain information which companies are required to provide under the Companies Act and other legislation and makes this information available to the public.

◼ Other useful terms

Articles of association	The document which contains the detailed internal rules of the company.
Charge	A means of securing a debt against an asset of the company.
'Crystallisation'	The process by which a floating charge attaches to specific assets of the company.
Derivative claim	An action brought by a shareholder on behalf of the company.
Fixed charge	A charge which is 'fixed' to a specific asset.
Floating charge	A charge which hangs over a class of company assets but does not attach until crystallisation.
Incorporation	The process of registering a company and creating a separate legal trading entity.
Limited liability	The ability of shareholders to 'limit' their liability for the company's debts to the amount which they have paid for their shares.
Listed company	A company which has its shares traded (or 'listed') on a recognised stock exchange.
Memorandum of association	The document which provides basic details of the company's status.
Negative pledge clause	A clause in the document granting a charge which prevents the company from granting another charge over the same assets.
'Off the shelf' company	A company which is purchased already registered.
Partnership	Two or more persons who trade together with no distinction between their personal and business assets.
Pre-incorporation contract	A contract which the promoters of the company make, before the company is incorporated, on the assumption that the company will assume responsibility for the contract.
Private limited company	A company which cannot offer its shares to the public.
Public limited company	A company which is able to offer its shares to the public by means of a prospectus.
Sole trader	A person who trades in their own name with no distinction between their personal and business assets.
'Veil of incorporation'	The theoretical barrier which separates the assets of the company from the assets of the shareholders.

Index

fiduciary 80, 83, 91
fiduciary, breach of 87
proper purpose 143
statutory 74, 75, 80, 91–2
employees, consideration of 90
environment, consideration of 90
power of to bind the company 64
powers, misuse of 75
register of 78
removal 74, 78
restrictions to appointment 70, 79
bankrupts 79, 80
disqualified persons 74, 79, 146, 147
mandatory disqualification 80
persons aged under 16 79
'shadow' 76–7, 143
and shareholders, imbalance of power and
knowledge between 91
disqualification (directors) 34, 74, 79, 80, 146,
147
duties *see under* directors

enlightened shareholder value 90
entrenchment 69
entrepreneurship 45, 56
equitable principles 80
see also just and equitable winding up
European Union law, influence of 56
external document *see* memorandum of
association
extraordinary resolution 133

'façade' companies 36–7, 141
family companies 120
finance *see* corporate finance and charges
Financial Services Authority (FSA) 24, 25
fixed charge 95, 96, 102, 103, 105, 107
floating charge 95, 96, 102–3, 104, 105, 107,
131–2
Foss v *Harbottle* rule 110, 111, 113–15, 118,
123
exceptions to the rule 113–15
fraud by those controlling company
115
personal rights of shareholder 113–14
special majority 114
ultra vires act 113

fraudulent trading 115, 147
limited liability and corporate personality 31,
34–5, 141
minority shareholder protection 145

Gazette (notice of registration) 19, 26
general commercial company model 63, 71
good faith 82, 83, 85, 119
goodwill 22
groups of companies 37–41, 44, 45, 141
guarantee, company limited by 7

holding company 37

identification theory 42
improper purpose, actions for 82
income tax 5
incorporation 6, 16–26, 140, 150
certificate of 19, 26
changing status of company 16, 23–5
company names 16, 17, 18, 19–23, 25
limited company 16, 18–19, 25
see also **'veil of incorporation'**
independent judgement (directors' duties) 84,
143
Industrial Development Consultants Ltd v *Cooley*
91
insolvency 126, 128, 132–4, 135
corporate finance and charges 95–6, 105,
107
directors 80
practitioner 128, 129
winding up 126, 132–4
insurance 32–3

judicial discretion to refuse application (winding
up) 145
'just and equitable winding up' 110, 111, 115,
120–2, 123, 132, 145
'quasi-partnerships' 120
when might a company be wound up
121–2

Kelner v *Baxter* 55

legal obligation, fulfilment of 64
legal personality 52